Classical
Korean Poetry

—more than 600 verses since the 12th century—

Selected and translated
with an introduction
by
Jaihiun J. Kim

ASIAN HUMANITIES PRESS
Fremont, California

ASIAN HUMANITIES PRESS

Asian Humanities Press offers to the specialist and the general reader alike the best in new translations of major works and significant original contributions to enhance our understanding of Asian literature, religions, cultures and thought.

Library of Congress Cataloging-in-Publication Data

Classical Korean poetry: more than 600 verses since the 12th century
/selected and translated with an introduction by Jaihiun J. Kim.
    p.   cm.
    Includes bibliographical references and index.
    ISBN 0-87573-056-6
    1. Sijo—Translations into English.   2. Korean poetry— To 1900—
Translations into English.   I. Kim, Jaihiun, 1934-
PL984.E3C38   1994
895.7'1008—dc20   94-31949
                                                                          CIP

Contents

Part III. The Golden Era

Part IV. The Dynasty in Turmoil

Part VI. The Kisaeng Class

Part VII. The Anonymous Works

Acknowledgements

Grateful acknowledgement is made to the Si-sa-yong-o-sa Publishers for permission to reprint portions of poems from my *Master Sijo Poems from Korea* (1982).

Also I gratefully relied on quoting some of Richard Rutt's annotations from his book *The Bamboo Grove*. My thanks go to Frank Concilus who kindly proofread my MS with helpful suggestions.

Foreword

Until about a hundred years ago Koreans wrote mainly in Chinese, as full members of what was to them the whole civilised world. They wrote Chinese with such competence and conviction that it was to them a not entirely foreign language. It rather, in some sense, played the role of a language for public use, while their own language was essentially for private use. What they wrote in Korean was addressed exclusively to fellow Koreans. Reading pre-modern literature in Korean is therefore a sort of eaves-dropping on private conversations between Koreans of the past.

So foreigners with an interest in learning what Koreans thought and felt among themselves in the past will be grateful to Professor Kim Jaihiun for easing their reading of this part of pre-modern literature in Korean, and for providing an historical context in which to set the works selected here. Whether that historical context is always factually accurate is an interesting study, but it is almost irrelevant, since that given here is the historical context in which the poems have been set by Koreans for nearly three centuries now.

An analysis of *sijo* as poetry can also be made. In setting the poems in their accepted historical context, Professor Kim describes how they deal with imagined events with liveliness and passion (to take David Daiches' admirably useful summary of Sidney's *Defence of Poesie*). The Korean language, in whatever literary form it is used, has its own poetry in this sense, and the question remaining is what particular poetry it has when it is versified.

Professor Kim sets out accepted Korean opinion on the subject clearly and concisely. This stresses the syllable count of the *sijo*, which is essentially a three-line version of the form which all pre-modern Korean verse used, and the sense structure found in the three lines. The western view will, I think, tend to lay stress on the grammatical structure of the poems and their diction. The match between the metre of the *sijo* and the grammar of the Korean language is remarkable: in other words the metrical structure of the *sijo* imposes just the lightest of disciplines on the natural structure of Korean speech, just enough discipline to make it poetry in verse rather than poetry in prose. The diction, the vocabulary, reflects the two traditions in Korea, that of China, the world of high civilisation, and that of Korea, the world of personal experience and emotion.

Finally there is the musical aspect of *sijo*. From the eighteenth century until the early years of the twentieth century the word *sijo* meant only a certain style of singing, and most of the pre-modern *sijo* poems which survive do so only because they were recorded in the notebooks of singers of the eighteenth and nineteenth centuries as suitable words for *sijo* songs. The world of Koreanology outside Korea still waits for the person who combines an enthusiasm for, and a competence in both *sijo* the music and *sijo* the verse. All are welcome to see whether they can perform that role, and it could be that they took their first steps by reading this anthology of Professor Kim Jaihiun's.

William E. Skillend
Emeritus Professor of Korean Studies
University of London
London, April 1993

Preface

The 600 verses (616 to be exact) presented in this anthology will provide the reader with comprehensive and varied aspects of the sijo, the traditional lyric, since its emergency as a fixed literary form as early as the late 12th century down to the 19th century. I have not included those pieces written after the 1900's, partly because of my belief that an historical evaluation of any work of art has to wait for the perspective of time, but chiefly because of my hope that recent works deserve due treatment in a separate volume.

In order to better give the reader a bird's-eye-view of the development of the sijo, I have broken down it into units of a hundred years or more for each period followed by works of the *kisaeng* and finally those by anonymous writers. When we think of history, we usually think of time-span characterized by certain events of importance. Sometimes the events are changes of dynasties, wars, social turmoil and introduction of alien thoughts from abroad. The sijo may or may not relate to the events. But there is a sense in which the sijo, like other works of art, cannot help relating in its history to history viewed as major events. The sijo must of necessity reflect in some way the tempers of the times in which it was written whether or not it proves unfit to that we think of as political, social and economic history. And thus I have attempted to arrange each sijo in a possible chronological order so that the reader can gain a glimpse at the sense of time, at the historical importance attached to a particular work. Yet, this is only a part of the whole. The genuine understanding of the traits and geniuses of a nation that has produced the works can be gained by looking at the whole picture as a whole.

In this anthology I am concerned with aesthetic quality of work, and yet I have not excluded those pieces, obviously didactic or Taoistic, because they have been in the main tradition of cultural heritage of Korea.

A few words on translation. My primary concern has been to be faithful to the original by giving as full a sense as possible. At times, however, it has been necessary that translation serves more as a kind of transmutation. From my experience, I believe word for word rendering in translating literary works rarely leads to satisfying results. What I have tried to achieve here has been to convey the spirit of the original, to be true to its vision. And naturally, a slight manipulation has been needed to make up for the loss of some mystic import given to a particular image in the original. Take, for example, the following by Chang, Hyŏn:

> After sundown over the Yalu,
> my lords, it pains me to see
> you dragging your feet all the way
> to Yenching ten thousand leagues away.
> When the new grass flames in spring
> may you return in no time.

The two princes Sohyŏn and Pongnim were taken hostage soon after Korea surrendered to the Manchus. The author followed them as an official interpreter. Under the circumstances, it is impossible to think that the princes were forced to walk all the way to China. It can easily be supposed that they were escorted in a palanquin or the like. In the same manner, the literal rendering of the original as "my pitiful lords" or "How I pity you, my lords," does not fit in with the context.

Technically, I have divided each line of each verse into two in translation simply for the convenience of visual arrangement. I have not spared a separate space for narrative pieces, usually longer than the standard ones. The number for each piece is put for the reader's reference to *Han'guk Sijo Sajŏn* (*A Dictionary of Sijo*) by Chŏng, Pyŏng'uk.

If any twists from the original resulted against my bona fide intentions, I am entirely to blame. I only hope that my undertaking will make some contributions toward expanding human consciousness and experience of beauty in the cross-currents of multiple cultures of the world today.

Jaihiun J. Kim
June, 1993
Seoul, Korea

Introduction to the
Classical Poems or the Sijo

I

The sijo is a traditional lyric of three lines or verses averaging 45 syllables in a stanza, each line made up of four phrase-groupings with a major pause after each grouping. This is not exactly the same as a caesura in English verse because it cannot be syncopated with metric feet. There is nothing in the sijo that can be accurately termed a metric foot, for it does not use accented stress nor syllabic length as a metric unit, although stress may contribute to the beauty of its rhythms.

Extremely elastic in form, the sijo differs from Chinese and Japanese verse forms in that it does not adhere to a strict syllable count. This is to say that there is considerable freedom of treatment of the basic pattern by the individual poet. Thus the number of syllables in each of the four phrase-groupings varied from two to five or more, but the variation in each part of the poem is different. Accordingly, the basic pattern of syllable count in the sijo is set down as follows:

First line	3	4	3	4
Middle line	3	4	3	4
Last line	3	6	4	3

On the other hand, Yi Pyŏnggi, the outstanding contemporary sijo poet and innovator, holds a theory which gives a different scheme because he prefers to ignore the secondary pauses in the first two lines. In many of the sijo, he believes, these pauses are so slight as to be virtually non-existent. His scheme indicates that the maximum number of syllable count for each half-line is not so great as the sum of the maximums of the component quarter lines. That is:

First line	6-9		6-9	
Middle line	5-8		6-9	
Last line	3	5-8	4-5	3-4

By comparison, Yi Ŭnsang suggests another scheme as follows:

First line	2-5	3-6	2-5	4-6
Middle line	1-5	3-6	2-5	4-6
Last line	5-9	4-5	3-4	

A comparison of the three tables show us the metric limits with which sijo has been written. From the tables, however, we can see a tendency for some phrase-groupings to remain constant or to maintain certain relations to one another as follows:

(1) The first group in the last line has invariably three syllables.
(2) The last group in the last line is most commonly of four syllables.
(3) The first groupings in the first and second lines are usually shorter than the one that follows.
(4) The second groupings in the last line is never less than five syllables.

A couple of examples will illustrate the scheme:

> hŭng-mang-i yusu-hani manwŏltae-do ch'uch'o-roda
> obaeknyŏn wang'ŏb-i mokjŏg-e puch'ŏsŭni
> sŏkyang-e chinanŭn kaeg-i nunmul-gyŏwŏ hanora

Poetically rendered it reads as follows:

> The rise and fall of things follow nature's way;
> autumn grass yellows on Full-moon Terrace.
> Five centuries of royal reign
> are drowned by the notes of a herdboy's flute;
> The traveler at dusk
> can hardly restrain his tears.

Another example is given of a poem by Yi Hwang, which corresponds to the regular scheme of 7(3-4), 7(3-4) in the first line, 7(3-4), 9(3-6) in the middle and 8(3-5), 7(4-3) in the last line. It reads in English translation:

> How is it that the blue mountains
> stay eternally blue?
> How is it that the running stream
> never ceases to flow day and night?
> We should also be like them
> and go on unchanged for all ages.

II

The form of the sijo is matched by its sense structure which is similar to that of a formal Chinese poem. The theme is stated in the first line, developed in the second and an anti-theme or twist is introduced in the third, which rounds out the whole in terms of resolution. If the first two lines consist of a query or question, the concluding line will answer or resolve it. Or it makes a neat comment often with a witty turn. The form of the sijo so far stated applies only to the standard form called plain sijo or *p'yŏng* sijo. The other two forms are called the medium or *ossijo* which is expanded in syllabic count, most often in the first phrase-grouping or the second in the first line and sometimes in the last. And the long sijo or *sasol sijo*, retaining a three-line structure, is almost formless expanded in every line and mostly in the middle into any number of syllables. In this book I have included not only the short plain sijo but also medium sijo, and long sijo which can be better classified as prose poetry regardless of its distinct line division. In fact, there has been much controversy as to whether it is considered sensible enough to break with the practice of the classical sijo in its formal syllable count. With the exception of modern writers, I wish to limit my attention to the standard form as far as the classical sijo is concerned.

III

The word *sijo* consists of two Sino-Korean characters meaning "time" or "period" and "rythmn" or "harmony," and it has been variously explained as referring to the seasonal significance of the song as is sometimes called the "song of seasons." Etymological data remain a matter of debate. Some scholars hold that the word sijo first appeared during the reign of King Ch'ungyŏl of the Koryo dynasty. However, it is generally accepted among most of the scholars including Yi Pyŏnggi that the word sijo was first used during the reign of King Yŏngjo (1734-1776) of the Yi dynasty and the widespread use of the word dates from the 1920's when Ch'oe Namsŏn, the pioneer of modern Korean literature, employed it in the title of an anthology. In the historical context, it was used as a musical appellation for a type of tan'ga or short song in place of sijo. As to the origin of tan'ga, later called sijo, there is no agreement of opinions. Some theorize that it originated in the early part of the Koryo dynasty, others ascribed its origin to the late or middle period of the Yi dynasty.

Since literature of a nation is a continuity of its culture, it follows that a certain literary form does not come into being overnight but comes to take shape through the long process of time. Among half a dozen of differing opinions, I take Yi Pyŏnggi's theory. According to him, the *tan'ga* was evolved from *hyang'a*, the native lyric of the Silla dynasty. It began to take its fixed form during the embryonic period in the middle of the Koryo dynasty when the form of *hyang'a* was gradually losing its influence. As in the world of Ch'oe Namsŏn that sijo is the optimum product of all the poetic heritages of the past dating back to short poems of the three kingdoms down to *kasa*, prose poetry typical of the Koryo dynasty, sijo poets must have seen in this particular type of short lyric an ideal vehicle to express what they had to say or felt. And with the invention of the vernacular alphabet in the early part of the Yi dynasty, the heritage of sijo came to take its roots firmly in the ground and enjoyed prosperity throughout the kingdom until its decline came in the beginning of the 1900's with the end of the dynasty.

IV

The characteristic or essential spirit of the sijo is sensibility expressed in the simplicity of naked emotion, often with a strong dash of witticism. Many of 3600 sijo as preserved in the classical anthologies constitute a commentary on history; on the events of social and political significance. It was also employed as a means of pouring out feelings and emotion of the public as well as formalistic norm and didactic precepts characterized by the Confucian society. In the earlier period it was mostly monopolized by the scholars and the nobility but with the propagation of *hang'ul*, the vernacular alphabet, the sijo came in the reach of all classes down to the kisaeng, the professional entertaining women on the lowest rung of the social ladder. Although the sijo now exists and is written chiefly as literature to be read, it occasionally enjoys being sung by sijo opera singers.

Part I. The End of the Koryo Dynasty

This period may justly comprise the era prior to the 15th century. As previously stated, it is an accepted theory that the sijo originated in the middle of the Koryo dynasty (918-1392) and began to take its definite form around the end of the dynasty. The sijo produced in this period were expressive of the mutability of human affairs, especially related to the decline of the kingdom, in addition to some of the immortal pieces regardless of the impacts of political changes. The major writers here represented, among others, are U T'ak, Yi Chonyŏn, Yi Saek, Yi Pang'wŏn, Chŏng Mongju, Wŏn Ch'ŏnsŏk and Kil Chae.

Ch'oe, Ch'ung (984-1068)

During the middle period of the Koryŏ kingdom, Ch'oe was the leading scholar of neo-Confucianism. He was called a Confucius of Korea. He left us with two poems, which must have been transcribed into the Korean alphabet, because they had apparently been written in Chinese. These poems are the oldest to appear in this anthology.

895

The sun sets duly in the west;
the yellow river empties into the East Sea.
The greatest men of all ages
all go to the graveyard in the end.
What can stop the rise and fall of things?
What's the use of regretting the inevitable?

1735

It is my life-long regret
that I was not born in the days of Fu-Hsi.*
Then, men wore garments of grass
and fed on wild fruits and greens
but their hearts were simple and true.
How I envy those peaceful times!

* Fu-Hsi was a legendary king in ancient China. He was believed to have taught men the art of fishing and other ways of living.

Yi, Kyubo (1168-1241)

A scholar in the latter part of Koryŏ dynasty, Yi wrote *The White Cloud Tales*. He also held some important military positions.

1730
The day is warm and the wind blows gentle.
The birds trill merry notes.
I lie down at ease in a yard
thickly covered with fallen petals.
Today the mountain abode is at peace;
there is nothing to bother about.

U, T'ak (1263-1343)

U was one of the first Koryŏ scholars to be concerned with neo-Confucianism. While most of the poems written by scholars are lacking in humor, U's work contains much humor and comical irony. He has two poems to his credit.

2270
Holding thorns in one hand
and a stick in the other,
I tried to block with thorns the road to age
and bat white hair with my stick.
But the grey hair knew better
and slipped by me taking a short cut.

2060
The spring breeze melted away the snow
on the hills and was quickly gone without a trace
Would that I borrowed it briefly
to blow through my hair;
I wish to blow away the ageing frost
thickening behind my ears.

Yi, Chonyŏn (1269-1343)

An outstanding scholar and poet of the late Koryŏ kingdom, Yi served four kings for nearly forty years at court. The poem given here is one of the rare examples of the allusive beauty of classical poems. The nightingale, a symbol of sorrow akin to that known in Western literature, here adds a melancholy zest to the beauty of a spring night. This is the only poem attributed to Yi.

1700

The moon beams white on the peach blossoms,
the Milky Way moored silvering at midnight.
I wonder if the nightingale has noticed
the spring spirit already alive in the branch?
I can hardly get to sleep
as if tenderness were a sickness.

Yi, Saek (1328-1396)

A distinguished Confucian scholar-official in the last days of the Koryŏ kingdom, Yi remained loyal to that dynasty during the turbulent times in which it succumbed to the rising Yi family. Despite his loyalty while serving his country, he suffered greatly when once sent into exile as a result of the factional strifes that plagued the court.

890

The clouds are lowering in the valleys
where the white snow lingers.
Where can the happy plum blossoms
be blooming, I wonder?
I stand alone in the evening sun
not knowing where to go.

Yi, Chono (1341-1371)

An historian of late Koryŏ times, Yi associated closely with Chŏng, Monju. He went through many reversals of fortune because of his straight-forward personality. He has three poems to his credit.

224

It sounds untruthful to say
that clouds have no minds.
Look how they float about in the sky,
following their own bents.
They doggedly chase the sun
trying to obscure its light.

Ch'oe, Yŏng (1316-1388)

A chief military commander in the late Koryŏ dynasty, Ch'oe was betrayed and later killed by his colleague Yi, Sŏngge, the founder of the Yi dynasty. Two poems are credited to him.

494

Let me fatten my prancing horse
and ride him, freshly washed in the stream;
sharpen my Dragon sword
and sling it over my shoulder;
I want to prove myself a man,
and pledge fidelity to my country.

516

Do not mock this pine tree,
bent low by the load of snow.
Can those flowers blooming in spring
endure forever in their beauty?
When the snowflakes drift by the wind
they will surely envy me.

Chŏng, Monju (1337-1392)

One of the most influential figures of his times, Chŏng played a major role as a special envoy to Ming China and Japan in smoothing Korea's precarious relations with those countries. The poem known as "The Fidelity Song" is perhaps the best known of all sijo. The poem was his answer to Yi, Pan'gwŏn's taunting piece. This poem gained even more fame after Chŏng was soon assassinated by the Yi faction for his refusal to support them.

1666

Though I die and die again,
though I die a hundred times,
though my bones turn to dust
and whether my soul exists or not,
what could change this single-minded
loyalty that glows toward my lord?

The mother of Chŏng, Monju (undated)

18

White heron, do not venture
into the valley where crows fight.*
The angry crows there will be
jealous of your whiteness.
I fear lest your clean-washed body
be stained with black.

* A legend says that Chŏng, Monju's mother composed this poem by way of warning his son against mixing with a group of power-greedy plotters who were planning to topple the existing Koryŏ regime and start a new dynasty, later named the Yi dynasty.

Cho, Chun (1346-1405)

Cho had served the last two kings of the Koryŏ kingdom before he joined the new regime, the Yi dynasty. He became Prime Minister under Yi, Sŏnggye, the founder and the first king of the Yi dynasty. He left us with two poems.

1258
Having had a drop too much I fell
asleep on the way on a deserted hill.
Who will rouse me from my sleep
pillowing on heaven and earth?
But a sudden gust of wind drives
home a fine rain and wakes me.

1133
Tipsy with wine toward twilight
I was plumped down on a donkey's back.
Ten leagues of hills and stream
passed as in a dream.
A few notes from a fisherman's pipe
suddenly woke me from a deep sleep.

Chŏng, Tojŏn (? -1398)

One of the leading scholars of the late Koryŏ kingdom, Chŏng played a major role in establishing the Yi dynasty. He wrote *A History of Koryo and Songs of a New Town*. He has one poem handed down to us.

1146
The waters that flow under the Fairy Bridge
pass through the village of Purple Mist.
That five hundred years of rule by this kingdom
should be reduced to the mere sound of water!
Come, boy, what sense is there in questioning
the rise and fall of the old dynasty?

Kil, Chae (1353-1419)

Kil was a schoolmate of Yi, Sŏnggye. When the latter became king, he sent for his old friend, who had resigned as Minister of Annals and retired to the countryside when the dynasty was in turmoil. Years later he made a lonely journey to the old capital of the regime. He has two poems to his credit.

1501

As I return on horseback to the town
where royalty reigned for five hundred years,
the hills and rivers seem the same as before
but great men and heroes are gone and seen no more.
How fleeting like a dream are
days of peace and calm!

Wŏn, Ch'ŏnsŏk (undated)

Wŏn left the court to live as a farmer in the country-side when the Koryŏ dynasty fell. The poem given here was composed when he revisited **Manwŏltae** after the new dynasty had moved the capital to Seoul. In this poem, like the one by Kil, Chae reminisces on things past, lamenting the brevity of human affairs, a common theme in literature. We are left with 2 of his poems.

2371

The rise and fall of things follow nature's way;
autumn grass yellows on Full-moon Terrace.
Five centuries of royal reign
are drowned by the notes of a herdboy's flute;
the traveler at dusk
can hardly restrain his tears.

515

Who would say the bamboo is bent,
snow-laden and bowing low?
If it were born to bend,
would it be greening in the snow?
Perhaps, bamboo, you are alone
in standing up to the cold of winter.

Yi, Pang'wŏn (1367-1422)

An important figure in the establishment of the Yi dynasty, Yi himself later
became King T'aejong. An eminent general, he was largely responsible for his
father's royal achievements. A legend says that Yi tried to win over supporters of
previous Koryŏ dynasty. He treated Chŏng, Mongju, the loyal subject of Koryo, to
a taunting toast at a party in an effort to persuade him to join the new regime.

1641

What does it matter
if you do something this way or that?
Who cares if the arrow-roots
grow tangled on Mansu Mountain?*
Why can't we be like those vines
and enjoy ourselves for a hundred years?

* Located in the outskirts of Kaesŏng, the capital of Koryŏ, the mountain has
seven Koryŏ royal tombs on it.

Part II. The Early Yi Dynasty*
(The 15th Century)

This period spans about another hundred years beginning with the foundation of the Yi dynasty to the era of King Sŏngjong. It is the period distinguished by the invention of the vernacular alphabet in 1443 by King Sejong. The bulk of sijo transmitted so far orally or remained in Chinese translation came to settle down in a fixed form. The period is also characterized by adopting Confucianism as a basis of national policy, exclusive of Buddhism. The sense of sorrow and grief over the old regime of the Koryo dynasty still dominated at the beginning of the period. With the initial turmoil of the new dynasty giving way to the calm of peacetime, some poets including Maeng, Sasŏng eulogized the time they lived in.

The usurpation of King Tanjong gave rise to a series of loyalty songs in the tradition of the one by Chŏng, Monju. The ensuing peaceful era during the reign of King Sŏngjong justly produced the peans of pastoral age. To the body of peace songs are added some patriotic ones by those in the military. Major poets of the period include Hwang Hŭi, Prince Wŏlsan, Sŏng Sammun, Yi Kae, Kim Chŏngsŏ and Wang Pang'yŏn.

* The Chosŏn dynasty is now officially accepted in place of the Yi dynasty.

Yi, Chik (1362-1431)

In the late Koryŏ and early Yi times, Yi served in a variety of posts including Minister of Interior and finally Prime Minister. One poem is credited to him.

15

Heron, do not laugh at the crow
because it is black.
Though black in appearance,
can it be black inside?
Perhaps, you are black at heart,
though white in appearance.

Hwang, Hŭi (1363-1452)

One of the most distinguished statesmen in the early part of the Yi dynasty, Hwang served four kings as Prime Minster and Ministers.

636

Are the chestnuts dropping in the valley
where the jujubes ripen red?
The crabs are out crawling
in the stubbled fields. Wine is being seasoned,
and a sieve-peddler is hawking his wares.
How can I resist testing the new wine?

101

With spring coming to the rivers and lakes
I have my hands full:
I must mend my fishing net first;
my boy is out plowing the field.
When will we have time to dig the medicinal herbs
that sprout up in the back hills?

1042

Can spring be late in coming
to my thatched hut by the clear stream?
The snowy masses of pear blossoms are fragrant;
the weeping willows glisten golden.
The nightingale trills in the misty valley;
enchanting spring thoughts have me in a daze.

Kim, Sang'ok (undated)

Under King Chŏngjo, Kim was a local military commander. One poem has
survived.

2057

Say, blue mountains, let me ask you,
for you know quite well, I believe,
the past and the present,
how many heroes have passed you by.
If any one after me should ask the same question,
add my name to your list.

Maeng, Sasŏng (1360-1438)

Despite his affiliation with the court, Maeng was well known for his integrity and
simple living. He was the Prime Minister of the Left under King Sejong. Maeng left
us with "The Song of Four Seasons," a cycle of four poems each depicting the
season of the year.

100

As spring comes to the rivers and lakes
a merry spirit irresistibly possesses me.
I amuse myself over wine
and fish to go with it.
This easy and free life of mine
is a favor granted by the king.

97

As summer comes to the rivers and lakes,
I have only to loaf in my thatched cabin.
There's no mistaking the river below;
the waves stir up a gentle breeze.
The fresh coolness I enjoy now
is a favor granted by the king.

95

As autumn comes to the rivers and lakes,
the fish are all fattened up and sleek.
I set my small boat adrift,
the fishing net flung into the water.
The freedom and leisure I have now
is a favor granted by the king.

96

As winter comes to the rivers and lakes,
the snow is piled more than a foot high.
I wear a wide-brimmed bamboo hat
and a mantle of dried rush.
This shelter from the cold
is a favor granted by the king.

Prince Wŏlsan (1454-1488)

Brother to King Sŏngjong, Wŏlsan was an outstanding poet of his times. He left us with one of the finest poems of pure lyricism in praise of nature. His real name was Yi, Chŏng.

231

With night settling on the autumn river,
the rippling waves are cold to the touch.
I fling a line into the waters
but there are no bites at all.
I paddle back in an empty boat
loaded with mindless moonlight.

Pak, P'aengnyŏn (1417-1456)

One of the court scholars commissioned to devise the Korean alphabet, Pak was later implicated in the Tanjong tragedy and was executed as one of the Six Martyrs. He wrote two poems concerning that tragic incident.

17

Caught in a drift of snow and sleet,
the crow appears white but is black.
Can the bright moon ever be
eclipsed by the dark of the night?
So shall my single-hearted loyalty to
our king never waver.

187

They say gold is mined in clear waters,
but can it be found in
any clear stream?
They say jade is quarried in the mountains,
but does every mountain yield it?
They say love means the most to us
but can we love all we meet?

Yi, Kae (1417-1456)

Like Sŏng, Sammun, Yi was one of the Six Martyrs. A great grandson of Yi, Saek of Koryŏ, Yi was also commissioned by King Sejong to devise the Korean alphabet. He left three poems behind him.

865

The candle that burns in the room,
from whom has it been parted?
While its outside drips with tears,
does it not know its heart burns?
The candle is like my own heart
and it does not know its heart burns.

Sŏng, Sammun (1418-1456)

Sŏng was one of the bright young scholars commissioned by King Sejong to devise the Korean alphabet. A major figure in the Tanjong tragedy, Sŏng and his followers remained loyal to the usurped King Tanjong. Defeated in their attempt to assassinate the usurper, later King Sejo, they were executed. They became known as the Six Martyrs. This tragedy inspired a number of loyalty songs. He left us with two poems, both alluding to the tragedy.

1665

What will I choose to be
when this frame of mine perishes?
I shall be a tall, spreading pine
on the highest peak of Mount Pongnae*
and when white snow fills heaven and earth
I shall stand upright, greening alone.

* The Diamond Mountains are called by this name in summertime. Perhaps, it was named after the sacred mountain in China.

1231

As I look at Shou Yang Mountain*
I grieve for Pai and Shuchai:
Why did they collect ferns for food
instead of simply starving to death?
On whose land did the greens
they tried to live on grow?

* Defeated in their effort to discourage their king from unjustly attacking Yin, in
ancient China, the brothers Pai and Shuchai quit the world and retired to Shou
Yang Mountain in the province of Shan Hsi and lived on a meager diet of ferns till
they finally starved to death. Our poet says he does not approve of their way,
because the mountain greens belonged to the land which the unjust king ruled.

Yu, Ŭngbu (? -1456)

Expert in archery, Yu was in the graces of Kings Sejong and Myŏngjong. Later he
was implicated in the Tanjong tragedy and was executed with 5 others. Yu was
one of the Six Martyrs. We have three poems by him.

61

Did the wind that raged last night
bring with it snow and frost?
Even the great spreading pine-trees
are all felled and blasted away.
How about those frail flower-buds
about to unfold?

1455

Did the wind that blew the other day
sweep down the rivers and lakes?
What has happened to the throngs
of boatmen caught out on the waters?
Long sequestered from the world
I do not know what goes there.

Yu, Sŏng'wŏn (? -1456)

A famed scholar in the royal court, Yu was one of the Six Martyrs executed for their opposition to the enthroning of King Sejo.

2110

Loafing under the thatched roof,
pillowing my head on my black harp,
I wanted to dream of
the piping times of peace.
But a fisherman plays tunes
at my gate and wakes me up.

Wang, Pang'yŏn (undated)

A courtier during the reign of King Tanjong and King Sejo, Wang was ordered to accompany the deposed Tanjong to his exile. Although as a official he had to perform this duty, Wang grieved in sympathy with the boy king. This poem concerns the incident.

1987

Ten thousand leagues away I left
my fair young lord, bidding him farewell.
I sit on the bank of a stream,
for I have nowhere to comfort my heart.
The water is like my heart,
and both weep through the night.

Wŏn, Ho (undated)

During the reign of King Myŏngjong, Wŏn was a member of the royal academy. After the boy king Tanjong was deposed by his uncle, later King Sejo, Wŏn resigned from official positions to retire to the countryside.

63

Last night I heard the stream
sobbing sadly as it flowed past.
Now that I think of it,
my lord must have wept for me to hear.
Would that the stream rushed backward
carrying my sorrow to him.

1284

I wish to be like the recluse T'ao Yin-ming*
who quit the world to live under five willows.
Then I take out a stringless harp
and play on it unheard strains;
the white crane in the yard knows the music
for he takes to footing joyful measures.

* Tao Yin-ming (365-427) was a famed poet and recluse in Chin, China. He was said to plant five willows around his house in the countryside.

Kim, Chongsŏ (1390-1453)

One of the outstanding generals of the Yi dynasty, Kim was responsible for garrisoning the north-eastern frontier and he earned his fame in history by pacifying the Nuchen tribes and settling what had been a disturbingly fluid frontier by setting the northern boundary along the Tuman-Yalu Rivers. Kim left us with two poems, both expressive of his undaunting military spirit.

1036
The north wind nips the bare tree-tops.
The moon shines cold on the snow.
Great sword held in hand I stand
in the frontier fortress far away,
whistling and shouting;
there's nothing to hold me back.

1786
Let me plant the flag on Changbaek-san*
and wash my horse in the waters of the Tuman River.
Look, effete scholars at the court,
isn't this the manly way to do things?
Whose portrait do you think should be
placed first in our Hall of Fame?

* Another name for Mount Paekdu, the highest in Korea.

Nam, I (1441-1468)

A son of King Taejong's daughter, Nam distinguished himself in subduing rebellions on the frontier. He was a Defence Minister at the age of 27 but was later killed by the opposition faction.

1780
With my long sword unsheathed
I stride up Mt. Paekdu* for a look around;
the rolling plains under the blue heaven
are being swept by the turmoil of war.
How long will it be before I defeat those barbarians
and peace will come to reign again in the land?

1814
I will fatten the prancing horse
and wash him sleek in the Tumen River.
I will draw my Dragon-sword from its sheath
and hold it shoulder high.
Let me hew out my fortune as a man
and hand down my name to posterity.

* The highest mountain in Korea.

Part III. The Golden Era
(The 16th Century)

This period, known as the golden era of literature spanning about one hundred years from 1490 to 1591, saw an abundance of sijo produced by a number of the most outstanding writers in the history of Korean literature. Despite the intermittent political disturbances, this period saw the sijo attain its summit as a nation's literary heritage. The decadence and factionalism that plagued the court found its expression in the writings of Cho Sik and Kim Inhu. The neo-Confucian philosophy which governed the thoughts of the times tended to develop the sijo toward ideological transmission rather than emotional expression of man. The tendency of didacticism in literature prevailed among the Confucian scholars. Yi Hwang, Yi I and Sŏ Kyŏngdŏk as major champions of new thoughts not only employed the sijo as a vehicle to propound their philosophy but also produced some of the finest works as works of art *per se*. Distinguished by vitality and grace of the vernacular, Chŏng Ch'ŏl's poems served to revolutionize Korean literature. It was at this time that a group of kisaeng left some poems which immortalized them. Hwang Chini, the best of them, lived during this period.

In 1592 the Japanese launched their first invasion into Korea and their second one in 1596 in an abortive effort for conquest. Major figures representing this period are Yi Hyŏnbo, Sŏ Kyŏngdŏk, Kim Ku, Kim, Koengpil, Song Sun, Yi Hwang, Cho Sik, Kim Inhu, Yang Saŏn, Sŏng Hon, Yi I, Chŏng Ch'ŏl, Kwŏn Homun, Cho Hŏn and Im Che.

King Sŏngjong (1457-1494)

He ascended the throne in 1496 as the ninth king of the Yi dynasty. He encouraged agriculture and sericulture as well as learning. *An Annotation of Tu Fu*, and *A History of Korea* were among his achievements. We have one poem by him.

1688
Why don't you stay longer?
Must you really leave?
Does it go against your grain to linger
or have you been talked into going?
Do what you may, yet do say something
for I am sad at heart.

* The king asks one of his favorite subjects to stay and serve him but the subject declines.

Kim, Koengp'il (1454-1504)

An outstanding neo-Confucian scholar, Kim was the victim of factional strife at court. He was a teacher of many of the brilliant scholars including Cho, Kwangjo. We have one poem by him.

1082
In a rain hat and rush-cape,
I pick up a hoe in the misty rain
to weed a hillside patch.
I lie down in the leafy shade
and a herdboy wakes me
as he drives home his cattle and sheep.

Yi, Hyŏnbo (1467-1555)

Yi was Privy Councillor under King Yŏnsan. Court strifes centering around the royal succession became violent at this time, plaguing the nation for the next hundred years. Distressed by this he took to nature to escape from the dusty world. Many of his poems were written in the tradition of the recluse Chinese poet, Tao Yin-ming. We have 9 poems by him.

226

I look down far into the green waters,
then look around at folded blue peaks.
What a place, sequestered from the world so
thickly coated with red dust!*
When the moon shines on the rivers and lakes
I am far from worldly cares.

* Red dust is a traditional symbol for the worldly cares and confusion.

265

"Return to the Fields" is but a cliché;
few actually return to the countryside.
Why should I stay here any longer
while the fields lie untended and barren?
The cool breeze strokes my thatched hut
waiting for its owner to return.

501

I mount the top of Deaf Peak;*
my old eyes can see better now.
Human affairs may shift and change,
but the mountains and rivers do not.
Those hills and heights before me
stand the same as I saw them yesterday.

* A reference to his pen-name Deaf-Peak.

1040

Clouds rise idly from the mountain peaks;
white seagulls fly about above the waters.
Both the clouds and the birds are
unconcerned yet full of devotion.
I will shake off my lifetime cares
and join them at play.

2104

The wind stirs the blue lotus blossoms;
I skewer the fish I've caught,
my boat tied to the reed-stalks,
their plumes bowing along the stream.
This clear and pure delight of mine
nobody will ever know.

1635

Among others, no worries of the world
come to bother this fisherman's life.
A leaf of a boat set adrift
on the waves of the boundless sea,
I have washed my hands of the world.
Who will ever know of my whereabouts?

Cho, Kwang-jo (1482-1519)

Skilled in calligraphy, Cho was a distinguished scholar-statesman during the reign of Kings Yŏnsan and Chungjong. His radical policies met with opposition that resulted in his death. He has two poems to his credit.

1851

That flat piece of rock over there
is where the angler-duke enjoyed fishing.
Where has the king, the fisher's friend, gone
leaving his fishing site unoccupied?
In the evening sun only a flight of swallows
skims over the wrinkling waters.

Sin, Kwanghan (1484-1555)

During the reign of King Myŏngjong, Sin was the Minister of Culture and Education. One poem is attributed to him.

1304

My mind is as limpid as a long river;
my body is as light as a floating cloud.
Free and idling on my own
I have white gulls to keep me company.
My only fear is that some mention of worldly
fame might fall on my ears.

Sŏ, Kyŏngdŏk (1489-1546)

One of the three greatest scholars of the Yi dynasty, the others being Yi, Hwang and Yi, I, Sŏ had no thoughts of gaining the favor of the court. Two poems are credited to him.

712

O heart, why is it that
you remain forever young?
Don't you know to also grow older
as I age with time?
Others may mock me, I fear,
for I strain to follow your beat.

713

Because my heart is foolish enough,
everything I do seems foolish.
Who will ever come to this remote mountain
hidden in piles of clouds?
Yet, falling leaves that rustle in the wind
make me think of her—perhaps, it's she.*

* The unidentified "she" is said to refer to Hwang, Chini, his talented disciple and kisaeng poetess.

Song, Sun (1495-1583)

During the reign of King Sŏnjo right before the Hideyoshi invasion, Song served the King as Prime Minister, from which position he resigned to live in the country-side. As pure poetry, Song's work is among the finest of this period. We have two poems by him.

2226
One day, as wind and frost nip the air,
fresh golden chrysanthemums
gathered in a silver vase
were royally presented to Jade Hall.*
Peach and plum blossoms, you cannot equal them.
We know how considerate the king is.

* The royal archives.

Hong, Ch'ungyong (1497-1547)

Hong became a local governor after serving King Chungjong in various capacities. One poem is left of his.

1892
The jade-blinds drawn half aside,
I look down into the green stream below.
Ten leagues of gleaming water
and the sky are the same color.
White seagulls circle in pairs
over the crawling waters.

Kim, Ku (1488-1543)

Kim was Vice-chancellor of the Royal Academy during the reign of King Chungjong. Unjustly framed as a ringleader in a political purge, Kim was sent into exile. After 13 years of exile, he returned to write "The Songs of Flowers." Kim was posthumously given the title of Vice-minister of Culture and Education. He has 5 poems to his credit.

1046

When the three-colored peach blossoms
float down the stream in the valley,
as I am naturally of a heroic spirit
I plunge into the water, clothes on
and come to the surface with flowers in my arms.

336

How happy I am today!
What a joyful day today—this day!
There is no other but the one today
the happiest day ever.
If each day to come should be like today
What cares could hold me back?

1538

Till the duck's short legs
change to the crane's
and the black crow turns
into the white heron
may good fortune attend you
and long life be yours forever.

1462

I wish here were there
and there were here;
so here is apart
from there, and there from here
I wish to become a butterfly
and come and go between them.

2195

Mount Tai is high, they say,
but it stands under heaven.
The ocean is deep, they say
but it lies upon the earth.
The benevolence of the king
must be high and deep indeed.

An, Chŏng (1494- ?)

During the reign of King Sŏngjong, An was a town magistrate. He was skilled in
drawing the "Four Sages" (the orchid, plum-blossom, chrysanthemum and
bamboo). We have two poems attributed to him.

1863

I ride my donkey all day
till it hobbles along at sunset.
The mountain path is steep and rough;
the stream purls down the ravine.
I hear the dog bark in the wind.
Here we are, home at last.

2075

Riding a blue ox* sidesaddle
I cross the green stream
on my way to dig elixir herbs
in the deep valley of Tie-t'ai-shan.
But all the valleys are folded in clouds;
I seem to have lost my way.

* Lao-tzu is said to have ridden a blue ox off into the west. Tien-t'ai-shan is a mountain in the province of Chekang in China. It is traditionally regarded as a center of Taoism.

Sŏng, Un (1497-1579)

After a brief public life, Sŏng retired to the countryside. Two poems of his work have survived.

1829

When spring comes to the fields
I have my hands full:
who will transplant the flower-trees
and plow the patch for medicinal herbs?
Boy, go and cut down some bamboos
and I will make my rain-hat first.

Cho, Sik (1501-1572)

Cho was a widely respected scholar whose reputation for honesty and candor became known while he was privy councilor to King Myŏngjong. But, like Yi Hwang, he left his office at court for the countryside to teach and meditate. The next poem describes his place of retirement. In all, he has 3 poems to his credit.

686

When I come to the stream in Mount Turyu
whose beauty I have long since heard of,
I see the mountains mirrored in the waters
dotted with floating peach blossoms.
Where is the fairyland, my boy?
This alone is the place.

1450

I wear hemp during the winter months
and dwell in a cave that keeps out rain and snow.
I have never basked through life
in the weakest rays of the sun.
Yet tears gather in my eyes
when I see it sink into the western peaks.*

* While in retirement he laments the death of King Chungjong. This piece is often attributed to Yang, Ŭngjŏng.

Yi, Hwang (1501-1570)

Better known by his pen name T'oegye, Yi was perhaps the greatest and most influential philosopher of the Yi dynasty. He held office at court but soon retired to the countryside where he studied and taught. Author of "The Twelve Songs of Tosan" which extolls in a cycle of twelve poems the beauty of nature, he concerned himself with the essence of human nature. We have 13 poems handed down to us.

1641

Should I do it this way?
Should I do it that way?
What if I should behave
like a rustic fool?
What can cure me of my
aching desire to return to nature?

1477

Let smoke and mist be my abode
and the winds and moon my friends.
While peace reigns in the land,
I grow old and weak with illness;
there's just one thing I ask of life:
to remain free from shame.

1616

The orchids in the valley
distil a sweet scent;
the white snow on the mountains
is a delight to the eyes;·
Far from the din of the world
I can hardly forget one gracious being.*

* A beloved beauty or the king.

1053

The terrace faces the mountains
and the stream runs down below.
Flocks of seagulls effortlessly
fly in and out.
My white pony, why do you think
of the far-away places?

503

The thunder may split the mountains
but it is not heard by the deaf.
The white sun may glow in mid-sky
but is not seen by the blind.
Blessed with keen ears and clear eyes,
we should not act as if we were deaf and blind.

145

Ancient man has not seen me,
neither have I seen him.
Though I have not seen him
I know what road he took.
Now that his road opens before us
should we not take it?

612

Many years have passed since
I last took to the road;
where have I been wandering,
straying from the road before this return?
I have come back now;
I'll never set my mind elsewhere.

2065

How is it that the blue mountains
stay eternally blue?
How is it that the running stream
never ceases to flow day and night?
We should also be like them
and go on unchanged for all ages.

1578

Isn't it an easy matter
for even fools know how to do it?
Is it not difficult
for even the sages do not fathom it?
No matter whether it is easy or hard
I wish to forget that I grow old.

2044

Only the seagulls and I know
Mt. Ch'ŏngyang's thirty-six peaks.
The seagulls will not tell;
but it is the peach-blossoms I distrust.
Peach petals, do not float far away;
I fear the fishermen will find us.

1999

Nestled against the Blue Cloud Terrace
my library is cool and clear.
A life-time of reading is
a joy without end.
What else can I ask, as I joyfully
ramble from place to place?

1237
Simplicity of manners dies out, they say;
but what they say is untrue.
Man is good by nature they say
and this time what they say is really true.
How could so many wits
of the world have been deceived?

Kim, Inhu (1510-1560)

Kim was one of the honored scholars in the Academy of Scholars which King
Sejong established in the early fifteenth century.

2055
The blue hills follow nature's way,
So do the green waters that flow.
Hills and waters go nature's way
And I follow it between them.
As I have grown up with both of them
So will I grow old following their way.

Yu, Hŭich'un (1513-1577)

A famed neo-Confucian scholar, Yu was exiled to Cheju Island for political
reasons.

816
I gather a bunch of Japanese parsley
and rinse it clean.
I did this for no one else,
only to give it to you.
What it tastes like isn't important;
just try it for my sake.

Yang, Saŏn (1517-1584)

Yang served forty-odd years as the magistrate of eight different districts. He has one poem to his credit.

2195

Though Mount T'ai* is said to be high,
it still stands below heaven.
If we kept climbing and climbing
we could surely scale its peak.
But without ever trying to climb the mountain,
people simply remark about its height.

* A sacred mountain in China, it is used as a symbol for any high mountain.

Song, In (1517-1584)

Song married one of the princesses during the reign of King Sukchong. Four poems of his work have survived.

2258

For thirty successive days this month
I have never gone without wine.
My hands do not hurt at all;
I do not suffer from hang-overs.
As long as my health holds out
I hope to remain quite unsober.

698

I forget things the moment I hear them;
I seem not to notice what I see.
This is the way life should be;
nobody will pick a quarrel with me.
My hands are strong and in good shape
and help me drink cup after cup.

1686
To say this or that alone hardly
makes anything happen.
Doing this or that in halves,
we let time slip by, unnoticed.
Why, what's once gone won't be back:
we should enjoy life while we can.

Hŏ, Kang (1520-1592)

Seeing his father sent into exile because of his integrity, Hŏ gave up worldly
ambitions and lived a simple life in the countryside. He has 8 poems to his credit.

773
The mountains tower higher and higher;
the long rivers flow without end.
I have to cover so many miles
along the rivers and across the hills.
When will my long sleeves dry,
ever-soaked with longing for my beloved?

Ki, Taesŭng (1527-1572)

Ki served King Sŏnjo as chairman of the Court Academy. We have one poem by
him.

2320
No one equals Prince Hsin-Ling
in luxury, wealth and fame;
yet in less than a hundred years
his grave was flattened into a field.*
What will become of others,
ordinary and common like us?

*An allusion to a poem by Li Po.

Kang, Ik (1523- ?)

During the reign of King Chungjong, Kang Ik retired to the countryside where he spent his days reading and writing. We have three poems by him.

1282

The dog barks at the brushwood-gate.
Who would come to this mountain retreat?
Some birds may be warbling
in the green bamboo grove.
There, boy, if anyone comes to see me,
tell him I've gone to gather ferns.

1924

To plant the orchids
I go out with a hoe over my shoulder
but the field is half-overgrown
with brambles and thorns.
Boy, I fear the sun will set
before we finish weeding.

Kwŏn, Homun (1532-1587)

Skilled in literary composition, Kwŏn retired to the country to enhance his learning. 19 poems are left of his.

1898

Should I go drinking and wenching?
Oh, no. It isn't proper for the poet that I am.
Shall I go hunting wealth and honor?
I am not inclined that way either.
Well, let me be a fisherman or shepherd
and enjoy myself on the reedy shore.

370

Day is done and dusk gathers;
I have no more work to attend to
and I bolt up the pine-wood door.
I lie down and relax in the moonlight.
No thought of this world comes
to bother me, not a speck of dust.

731

Repeatedly, I try to resign my position,
cleanly cutting these worldly ties.
If I need not bother about it
I will find freedom and leisure.
Even now I can see what I have done so far
is not right as it should be.

983

Though far out of reach,
the green woods and spring-well enchant me.
Unconcerned, the fish and the birds
delight in their natural freedom.
Before long I will put aside
the whole of my worldly cares to join them.

1157

The way the sages take remains
the same since antiquity.
Whether it is hidden from view
or revealed, clear to our sight,
there's only one path to be sought.
Whether I live here or elsewhere
makes no difference at all.

1842

The clear moon disperses the clouds,
rising over the far-away timber-line.
It is so bright, shining
upon the green stream below.
A flock of seagulls from nowhere
flies in a wingbeat and follows me.

1379

When it stops raining at the fishing site
I will use green-moss for bait.
With no idea of catching the fish
I will enjoy watching them at play.
A slice of moon passes as it casts a silver line
onto the green stream below.

Yi, Wang'wŏn (1533-1592)

Yi studied under Yi, Hwang, the great master of neo-Confucianism. He was the
Prime Minister during the reign of King Sŏnjo. He left one poem behind him.

479

After you've talked me into climbing
to the top of a giant tree,
hear me, my friends down on the ground,
do not try to shake me down.
I am not sad that I perish in a fall;
I fear lest I meet my beloved.

Yu, Chasin (1533-1612)

The father-in-law of King Kwanghae, the 15th king of the Yi dynasty, Yu served the king as Vice Minister of Culture and Education. He has one poem to his credit.

2138
The autumn mountains sink into the river,
tinted red by the setting sun;
I sit alone in my little boat
with a bamboo fishing rod.
Seeing me free and unburdened
the heavenly Duke sends me a bright moon.

Ko, Kyŏngmyŏng (1533-1592)

A scholar versed in literary composition and calligraphy, Ko rallied the militia to fight back the Hideyoshi army and was killed in battle during the reign of King Sŏnjo. 3 poems are attributed to him.

921
When I see her, I hope she will turn me away;
if I don't, I hope I will forget her.
Would that she had not been born
or that I had not known her.
I'd rather perish straight away
leaving her longing and pining for me.

2053
My Blue-dragon sword on my shoulder,
I will throw myself on a white deer.
I range over the hills and down the waters;
the sun sets behind the mulberry patch.
The clear sound of a bell from the fairy court of the immortals
rings far through the clouds.

1940

I tie up my boat on the shore of the Chinhwe River
and find way into a wine shop near the waterfront.
The hostess doesn't know
the nation is about to ruin;
She's chanting an obscene tune
while mist blurs the river, sand sparkles in the moon.

Sŏng, Hon (1535-1598)

An outstanding scholar of neo-Confucianism, Sŏng served King Sŏnjo as the Vice Minister of Defence. Despite his philosophical differences with Yi, I, they were great friends. He has three poems to his credit.

1289

In this piping time of peace
I loaf my days away in the country.
But for the cock, crowing at noon
in the greening bamboo groves,
who will come this far to wake me
from a fairy's dream.

733

The blue mountains have no speech;
the running waters have no form.
The clear wind can be had for nothing;
the bright moon has no owner.
Among these, I shall grow old,
free from illness and worries.

Yi, I (1536-1584)

Better known by his pen name Yulgok, Yi is another great Confucian philosopher of the Yi dynasty. He is the author of "The Nine Songs of Kosan" which depicts in a cycle of nine poems the beauty of the place he returned to to make his home. We have twelve poems by him. The nine songs were modeled in setting on "The Nine Songs of Wui" written by Chu Hsi, the noted neo-Confucian thinker of China while he dwelled in Wuishan in Fu-Chien province.

142
The nine bends in Kosan*
are unknown to the world.
I've built there a cabin of grass
and my friends come to see me.
Here I think of Wui-shan
and read the master Chu Hsi.

* A mountain located in Hwanghae province, now in North Korea.

1729
Where is the first bend of water?
The sun shines on Crown Rock.
The mist clears from the fields.
Far and near, lie landscape paintings.
I set the wine jar under the pines
as I wait for my coming friends.

1633
Where is the second bend?
Late spring welcomes Flowery Rock.
Let me toss flower-petals down
into the green ripples of the stream.
The world does not know of this place.
What matter if I tell of it?

1070

Where is the third bend?
Leaves thicken on Emerald Screen.
The birds are warbling in pitches
low and high in the foilage.
Light wind fans the dwarf pines
and summer seems out of place.

993

Where is the fourth bend?
The sun sets over Pine Cliff.
The rocks are many-hued, mirrored
in the waters of the tarn.
The woods and spring water are deep and quiet.
I cannot suppress my mirth.

1484

Where is the fifth bend?
A hidden screen commands a wonder-view.
My retreat by the stream
is cool and pleasant.
Here I can teach young men
and converse with nature as well.

1624

Where is the sixth bend?
Waters spread smooth in Fishing Gorge.
There the fish and I are at play
competing with each other for joy.
I shoulder my fishing rod
and return home in the moonlight.

2173
Where is the seventh bend?
The rocks luxuriate in autumn tints.
The frost forming on the cliff-sides
makes for embroidered silk all around.
I sit alone on the cold rock
forgetful of returning home.

2207
Where is the eighth bend?
The moon beams on Lute Rapids.
Here I will play a few tunes
on a jade lute.
Nobody knows the ancient strains
so I alone delight in them.

216
Where is the ninth bend?
The year comes to an end on Mt. Mun.
Rocks of fantastic shape are
all buried under the snow.
Now nobody ventures to come this far;
they say there's nothing to see.

Chŏng, Ch'ŏl (1536-1593)

Chŏng studied under Kim, Inhu and Ki, Taesŭng and associated with scholars like Yi, I and Sŏng, Hon. As a leader of the political faction called the West Men, he naturally met with many reversals of fortune. Apart from politics, however, Chŏng is remembered as one who helped bring classical poetry to the summit of artistic perfection. Along with Yun, Sŏndo, another giant of classical literature, Chŏng's contritutions to the Korean poetical heritage are unsurpassed. Besides his Samiin-gok (A Song of Love), a masterful prose poem, more than ninety poems have survived.

317
Two stone buddhas by the roadside
face each other, naked and unfed.
Though they stand unprotected
against wind, rain, snow and frost,
I envy them because they do not know
the pain of separation.

1632
There, old man, let me
carry your load.
I am young, and even a rock
is light for me.
Age itself is a sorrow;
why burden it with such a load?

1811
Yesterday I was told farming official Sŏng
across the hill had wine mature enough to drink;
I kick my idle cow up to its feet
and get into the saddle.
Come, boy, is your master in?
Tell him County head Chŏng's come.

1221
Snow has fallen on the pine-woods,
and burst them into blossoms
I would like to pluck one branch
and send it to where my lord is.
After he has seen the flowers
what does it matter if they melt away?

1858
Pine tree standing by the roadside,
how is it you stay there?
Can't you step back a little
and stand in the ditch?
Everyone with rope and axe
is tempted to strike you down.

2232
Where have all the boats gone,
tossed about by the winds and waves?
Did they venture out to the sea
when the dark clouds lowered?
All of you whose boats are not sea-worthy,
take heed of my warning.

419
If only I could cut out my heart
and fashion it into a bright moon,
suspended on high
in the vast spread of heaven,
I could go where my beloved is
and shine brightly on him.

1392

Huge timbers for roofbeams and pillars
have fallen into disuse.
While the house is about to collapse
they are in the heat of an argument.
Carpenter, how long will you putter about
with your rules and inkpot.*

* Formerly, a length of thread was blackened to draw straight lines.

1911

Ten years have passed since I last saw
the white jade cup in the royal archives.
Its white and clear color remains
the same as it was before.
Why is it that man's heart is so fickle,
changing from morning to night.

1485

The day has dawned again.
Let's take hoes to work in the fields.
After I am through with my field,
I'll go and hoe yours.
On the way back we can gather
mulberry leaves for the silkworms.

624

The shade-tree stands on the terrace.
How long since I planted it?
Once a sappling shot up from a seed,
it has grown into a giant zelkova.
Now, let me offer it a cup of wine
for it's lived so long.

464
How much progress has your son made
in mastering *The Book of Filial Duty*?
My son will finish his primer
the day after tomorrow.
How long I wonder before he'll
master the classics and be a decent man?

1101
Appointed the new magistrate at Saewŏn,
I have so many callers.
As they come and go,
I have to greet them and see them off.
Left to myself at times,
I think how tiresome my job is.

1386
While your parents are alive
do well by them as a son should.
After they are gone and are no more
what will be the use of your regrets over them?
The lost chance to serve them
cannot be redeemed for life.

1776
The birds are returning to the nest
and the new moon rises.
There, Zen-priest, crossing
a log over the stream,
how far is your hermitage
that I can hear the distant sound of its bell?

1264

The soup of bitter greens
can taste better than meat.
The thatched hut is small,
which matches well with my lot.
I miss you beyond words
and it makes me so sad.

1318

My father gave me life,
my mother nourished me.
Were it not for them,
I could not have come into being.
Their love for me cannot be repaid;
it is as boundless as the sky.

2261

Man and wife are made from one body
divided in halves.
They live and age together
and become united in death.
What a shame some vicious souls
scowl at the loving couple!

1745

If we were given a hundred years to live
we would still bustle and make a fuss.
What can be done in a life as
fleeting as a floating cloud?
Then do not refuse again
this cup of wine I offer you.

331

When a tree catches a disease
the arbor below is useless.
When it gloried in green foliage
passers-by came for the shade;
when the branches go bare, its leaves gone,
not a single bird comes to it.

2081

O crane that used to wing across
the blue heaven above the clouds,
why did you come down to earth?
Because your heart warmed to things human?
You must have forgotten how to soar
with your long feathers almost fallen off.

2370

Things rise and fall ceaselessly;
autumn grass yellows in the fortress.
Let all things past be buried
in the notes of the herdboy's flute.
What does it matter if I have a drink
in this piping time of peace?

2313

Brothers, elder and younger alike,
touch every part of your body
and you will see you are framed alike,
fathered from the same root.
You have grown nursing on the same breast.
Never be unkind to each other.

51

As a man turns aside
for a woman to pass,
a woman steps aside from the road
for him to proceed.
Neither should ask the other's name
if they are not man and wife.*

* An ancient custom.

1223

A sudden rain showered down
on the lotus leaf
but the leaf leaves no trace
of rainwater on it.
I wish my soul could be like it,
going untouched by dirt.

144

I tried hard to stifle my feigned laugh
and instead I sneezed violently.
Make-believe affection goes sour
and loses love which is full and true.
We must not be drawn to wine
which is not yet fermented.

751

Paulownia leaves are dropping
and I know autumn is here to stay.
A thin rain falls on the clear stream
and the night air is cool.
But my beloved is a thousand leagues away
and I lie awake, unable to sleep.

2340
Swallowtails flutter in pairs
over the glittering flowers.
Orioles in company sing duets
in the greening weeping willows.
There's no creature that doesn't pair off.
Only I remain alone.

1295
This pagoda has endured
eight centuries of the Silla dynasty.
The great bell weighing a thousand pounds
booms in waves far away
and vibrates in the clear air over
the deserted bower across the hill.

1103
As the new magistrate at Saewŏn,
I mend my brushwood gate.
As if in exile I keep friends with the running
stream and the blue mountains.
Boy, if anybody comes for me,
tell him I'm not in.

2281
"A Drinking Song"

Let's have a drink and then have another.
Let's pluck flowers and count off each petal
to match the endless cups of wine.
Once this frame of ours is dead it will be
rolled up in a straw mat and carried away
on an A-frame or borne in a flowery bier
mourned by the whole village.
But once it has passed through the reeds and
rushes and white aspen,

where the sun slants ye'low
and the moon shines white;
where thin rain falls
and snow swirls in heavy flakes;
where the whirlwind howls
then who will say, "Let's have a drink?"
And, when monkeys come to chatter
on your grave, what good will it do
to regret?

Sŏ, Ik (1542-1587)

During the reign of King Sŏnjo, Sŏ was a local magistrate. After retirement from public service he remained loyal to the king.

497

A horse unbridled and set free
on the bank thick with green grass,
I lift my head from time to time
and neigh aloud to the north.*
With the sun setting behind the hills
I long in tears for my beloved lord.

* The north indicates where the king resides.

1674

Should I level this hill
and fill up the rolling ocean
so that I can walk as far as Pongnaesan*
and meet my beloved there?
But like the legendary sandpiper**
I just roam about by the shore.

* One of the sacred mountains in China where immortals and fairies live on elixir herbs.
** Legend has it that a lovely prince turned into a sea bird after death.

Im, Che (1549-1587)

Im is remembered as one of the few theorists who stressed a more independent course for Korea at a time when Korea accepted suzeranity. Also famous as a ladyman, he loved Hwang, Chini and Hanu.

2087
Are you asleep or just resting
in that mound covered with green grass?
Where have those rosy cheeks gone and
do mere bones lie buried here?
I hold a cup but I am sad
for I have no one to whom I can offer it.

965
The northern sky would clear up, they said.
So I set out without a raincape.
But snow was falling in the mountains
and cold rain* fell in the fields.
Today I was soaked by the cold rain
and tonight I shall shiver, frozen, in my bed.

* This piece is called Cold Rain song. It makes a pun on the name of kisaeng named Hanu or Cold Rain, who replied to the poem with her own.

Han, Ho (1543-1605)

Better know by his pen name Sŏkbong, Han was one of the master calligraphers of the Yi dynasty. One poem has survived.

1942
Do not bother to spread the straw-mat.
Can't I sit on the fallen leaves?
No need to light the pine torch;
the moon rises that sank last night.
Now, boy, get me a cup of wine
with some mountain greens to go with it.

Cho, Hŏn (1544-1592)

Cho organized a local militia to fight back Hideyoshi's army and was killed in action. Posthumously he was raised to the rank of Minister of Justice under King Sŏnjo and later to Prime Minister under King Yŏngjo.

1921
The rain patters on the lotus pond;
thin smoke wreathes the weeping willows.
The boatman has disappeared, I know not where,
leaving his empty boat moored to the bank.
A lone seagull flies to and fro
against the glow of the evening sun.

2213
The wild geese settle on the sandy flats.
Dusk invades the riverside hamlet.
Snowy seagulls are quiet asleep.
Fishing boats are on their way home.
Notes of a flute wafting from somewhere
seize me with a merry spirit.

1948
I sit carefree in my drifting boat,
a line cast into the green waters.
In the evening sun I delight in the rain
that patters on the bank of the clear river.
Let me get a willow branch
and skewer the fish I've landed.
We'll head for the wine shop in the village.

Part IV. The Dynasty in Turmoil
(The 17th & 18th Centuries)

Ranging from 1592, the 25th year of King Sŏnjo's reign to 1720, the last year of King Sukchŏng of the Yi dynasty, this period saw the country plunged into a turmoil from within and without. The two great invasions by the Japanese and the Manchus laid the country completely waste. And the internal strifes among the differing political factions conspired to make the situation worse. Under the circumstances, a recurring theme of futility and despair prevailed among the people overwhelmed by the catastrophic events. The poet saw that destiny is not shaped by man but by forces out of man's control. He saw no constancy in human situations and resigned himself to the mutability of things and evanescence of life. Man is a creature incapable of bearing reality; he must overcome despair through creating an illusion of reality of his own. Driven by the eternal forces of history he escaped into the impersonal bosom of nature or turned to a life of wine and sensual pleasures. And in the middle of musings on his fate, he turned his eyes inward to illumine humanity as a whole. At last he learns how to remain calm and quiet.

Most important, this period saw an emergence of the middle class writers as a dominant literary force. A series of foreign invasions, of course, contributed to exposing the incompetence and helplessness of the ruling class, awakening in the general public a sense of their own identity. Naturally the tones of the sijo underwent change from idling with ideas to probing realistic life. Despite the aftermath of devastating wars, however, this period found one of the few consummate artists in Yun Sŏndo. Yun was undoubtedly the finest poet of the classical sijo in the same way Chŏng Ch'ŏl was that of *kasa*, classical prose poetry. Yun succeeded in polishing the vernacular to its highest grandeur and in exploiting the Korean language to the full for its poetic possibilities. Again, though in a lesser degree, Sin Hŭm and Pak Inno played a considerable part in enhancing the quality of national literature. The major poets included in this period are Cho Hŏn, Yi Sunsin, Kim Tŏknyŏng, Han Ho, Kim Changsaeng, Chang Man, Sin Hŭm, Pak Inno, Yi Myŏnghan, Kim Sanghŏn, Kim Kwang'uk, Kim Yuk, Yun Sŏndo, and Nam Kuman.

Yi, Sunsin (1545-1598)

Yi turned the tide of Asian history by decisively defeating the Japanese fleet launched by Hideyoshi in 1592.

2267

On this moonlight night on Hansan isle
I sit alone in the lookout.
Great sword worn at my side,
I am weighed down by worries.
From somewhere the sad notes of a flute
rend my heart.

Kim, Changsaeng (1548-1631)

One of the students of Yi, I and later a great scholar in his own right, Kim retired voluntarily from official life to the countryside where he taught, establishing himself as a leading figure of neo-Confucian philosophy. He has one poem to his credit.

632

I'll plant bamboos to fence in my hut
and grow pine-trees to serve as a bower.
Who'll ever know that I live here
submerged in the silvering mist?
The crane that stalks about in the yard
is the best friend I have.

Yi, Wŏnik (1547-1634)

During the reign of King Sŏnjo, Yi served as Prime Minister of the Left and Right as well as Prime Minister. He has one poem to his credit.

491
Can a thousand threads of willow
tie up the parting spring?
Can bees and butterflies
keep flowers from fading away?
No matter how deep my love is,
how can I stop my beloved from going?

King Sŏnjo (1552-1608)

The fourteenth king of the Yi dynasty, King Sŏnjo had, among others, the very best of scholars, Yi, I and Yi, Hwang, serving for his court. His reign was plagued by the Hideyoshi invasion. He has one poem to his credit.

1500
When he arrives he is ready to leave;*
when he departs, his return is uncertain.
Coming and going, he is
rarely seen for long.
Today he is leaving again
and it saddens my heart.

* The king misses one of his favorite subjects who shuns serving at court.

Yi, Hangbok (1556-1618)

Yi was Prime Minister of the Right under King Sŏnjo. He distinguished himself
during the Hideyoshi invasion. We have 4 poems by him.

104

Since I made that promise to return to the lakes
I have been bustling about for ten years.
The white seagulls may say I am late,
but they do not know why.
I was graced with the king's favor
and I felt obligated to loyally serve him.

2031

O clouds that pause before crossing
over the high Ch'ŏllyŏng peak,
behold me, I weep in mortification and solitude.
Make a rain of my tears
and sprinkle it over the royal court
where my lord the king resides.

Cho, Chonsŏng (1553-1627)

Cho served King Sŏnjo during the Hideyoshi invasion in 1592. When the Manchus
invaded during the reign of King Injo, Cho escorted the prince to safety in the
countryside. Here are four of his poems.

1329

Come, boy, take up your mesh-bag;
dusk gathers on the western hills.
Fernheads will soon unfold
and wilt overnight I fear.
What should we have for breakfast and supper
were it not for the greens?

1331

Come, boy, gather up the reed-cape and bamboo-hat;
the rain has stopped by the east creek.
On my long fishing rod,
we'll fix a barbless hook.
Fishes, don't take fright,
I am here just for the fun of it.

1333

Come, boy, fix me some porridge for breakfast;
much work awaits in the south field.
I wonder who will lend me a hand
while I struggle with my clumsy plow.
Let it be. We can take it easy
by the grace of the king.

1332

Come, boy, feed the cow and get her ready;
I'll ride to the north for some new wine.
When I ride home in the moonlight
with my face flushed red with drink
who can I be tonight other than
the Emperor Fu-Hsi riding home?*

* A legendary king in ancient China.

Pak, Inno (1561-1642)

Along with Chŏng, Ch'ŏl and Yun, Sŏndo, Pak is regarded as one of the three greatest poets of the Yi dynasty. Author of "The Song of Peace," Pak was a devoted son who pursued the cardinal virtue of filial duty. In fact, most of his 70 surviving poems concern Confucian themes treated didactically.

855

The luscious red persimmons on a dish
are beautiful indeed.
Though they are not pamelos,*
I would tuck them in my pocket;
but I have no one at home to enjoy them
and it makes me sad.

* It is an allusion to an ancient Chinese episode in which a boy noted for his filial piety brought his parents some pomelos given to him at a wealthy family. Pak's poem implies that his parents are dead, no more able to enjoy the fruit.

1092

The new moon has just come up over the back hills
and is beaming her light onto the floor.
The air is full of beating wings
as birds search out their nests.
The monk is crossing the log
that spans the stream.
You say you can hear the evening bell
of your hermitage from here?
How far can it be?

1436

Well, boys, come along,
cleanly cut the ties of the dusty world.
The fields in the country lie waste;
there's no time to lose.
The moon and cool wind beckon
us down the clear stream at home.

342
I stroll down to the shallows,
my fishing rod held aslant in my hand.
I push the redshank aside for a seat
and sit in the moonshine.
What joy in this world
could ever compare with mine?

393
No union is more precious
than man and wife being in wedlock.
All the bliss life can offer
culminates in conjugal love.
Therefore, the harmony of the couple
is to be most sought after.

662
We are brothers three in all,
living as one body and flesh.
But two have gone, I know not where;
they are still away from home.
Every evening, leaning upon my gate,
I sigh for my brothers.

1214
There, you boys at play beneath the pine-trees,
where have your elders gone?
They went digging medicinal herbs;
it's about time they were home.
But a thick mist has covered the mountains
where they are now we cannot tell.

935

The moon rising over the mountain peak
shines on the mountainside.
The sky spreads high and distant,
ninety thousand leagues long.
Almost high enough to scrape the sky,
I feel I fly over that peak.

976

From far away though, how far can it be?
Drums are beating in a temple
that must be on some blue hillside
beneath the fleecy clouds.
But the mist thickens again today;
I cannot see where it might be.

722

Would that I could melt down ten thousand pounds
of iron and beat out into a great length of rope
to tie up the sun that races
across the vast heavens
so that my white-haired parents
at home would age slowly.

Kim, Sang'yong (1561-1637)

Kim served Kings Sŏnjo and Kwanghae in the capacity of royal secretary and Minister of Justice. When the Manchu army seized the Kwanghwa fortress, the last stronghold of Korea, Kim committed suicide. We have 4 poems by him.

1496

Unconcerned, I hear the rain
patter on the paulownia.
My heart is sad, and no wonder,
each rain-drop on the leaves brings sorrow.
After this, I would never
plant a broad-leafed tree.

286

The incense has burned out in the golden incensor.
The water in the water-clock has run dry.
Where have you been?
To whom did you make love?
Now a shaded moon slanting on the balustrade,
you've come back to see how I feel.

740

If you speak, you are called brash;
yet silence makes you a dummy.
Poverty is laughed at;
but riches and fame attract jealousy.
Indeed it is not easy
to live in this world.

1013

Love is a lie,
so is your love for me.
Your pledge to visit me in my dreams
is still another lie.
Lying forever awake as I do,
how could I ever hope to see you in a dream?

Yi, Tŏkhyŏng (1561-1613)

Yi served Kings Myŏngjong and Kwanghae in the capacity of Prime Minister. He
has four poems to his credit.

599

The moon is round, suspended
in the jade spread of sky.
It may plummet any minute,
battered by frost and the winds of time.
But right now I want it to shine
for me on my golden drinking cup.

2179

Filling my cup to the brim,
I empty each till I get drunk.
I count on my fingers
how many heroes we have had.
Of them all both Li Po and Liu Ling
are my greatest friends.

Yi, Chŏnggui (1564-1635)

Skilled in literary composition, Yi was Prime Minister of the Left and of the Right during the reign of King Injo. He has one poem to his credit.

570

Can I trust you, my love?
No, you're not to be trusted.
I've long trusted you,
though I've known you are untrue.
But as hard as it is to believe you,
what else can I do but keep trusting?

Kim, Tŏknyŏng (1567-1596)

Kim organized a militia to fight the Japanese during the Hideyoshi invasion. He was falsely charged by his political enemies and imprisoned. The following poem is said to have been written prior to his death.

2149

With the spring hills on fire
all the buds burn unflowered.
We have the water
to quench this fire.
But the smokeless fire blazing in my heart
no water can extinguish.

Kim, Sŏng'wŏn (? -1597)

During the reign of King Sŏnjo, Kim was a local governor. He exhorted the militia's fight against the invading Hideyoshi army. We have one poem by him.

468
The passing clouds are cross and wilful
enough to obscure the bright moon.
I have no choice but to sit alone
and it grieves my heart.
Happily, the wind reads my mind
and pours down a wash of rain.

Yang, Ŭngjŏng (undated)

Yang was the chairman of the Royal Academy during the reign of King Myŏngjong. He has two poems to his credit.

2202
In the piping time of peace,
a chipbox and a gourd strapped on my back,
my long sleeves billowing in the wind,
I lope along my carefree way.
Nothing bothers me in this world.
I am merry and gay.

Sin, Hŭm (1566-1628)

A leading scholar-official during the reigns of Kings Sŏnjo and Injo, Sin eventually
sought refuge in the countryside far from the court intrigues. He has 31 poems to
his credit.

1061
Snow has fallen on the mountain village
and the stone path is buried under the snow.
Do not open the brushwood-gate;
who will come this far to see me?
A slice of moon shining in the night
is the only friend I have.

473
The man who made a song
must have known many sorrows.
He must have realized that words alone
could not free him from his cares.
If singing could chase my sorrows away
how gladly I would sing!

52
It rained during the night
and the pomegranate has broken into blossom.
I hitch up the crystal blinds
of the pavillion by the lotus lake:
how I wish to unload this sorrow
caused by someone I love.

2310

Be the rafters long or short,
the pillars bent or warped,
do not mock my thatched hut
because it is so small.
Look, how the hills and trees
gleam in the moonlight. Aren't they all mine?

368

Do not ask what I am.
I used to be a minor official.
How long has it been, I wonder,
since I rode away on a blue ox.*
The world is a whirligig.
I feel out of place.

* Reminiscent of Lao-tzu.

457

Egret by the brookside,
what are you standing there for?
You must be watching the fish
for a chance, aren't you?
Don't you think you should give up?
You share with them the same living space.

190

What are honor and fame
but worn-out shoes?
Now I'm back home in the fields,
deer and fawns keep me company.
If I may go on like this for a hundred years,
it is by the grace of the king.

380
Let me plow a strip of land
on the slope of distant South Mountain
and visit Mount Samsin
to dig for the herbs of immortality.
Then I shall boast that I'll live to see the seas
dry up into a mulberry patch.

1241
I do not say it is good to drink your days away.
Don't you know Duke Sin Ling's tomb
was flattened into a cornfield?
Life of a hundred years
is plagued by trouble and distress;
why don't you drink up and enjoy yourself?

159
Leaves break into green, flowers faded;
one season gives way to another.
Green caterpillars in the leafage
are transformed into fluttering butterflies.
Who is the magician, give me his name,
that work these wonders?

410
Would that I painted a picture of my beloved
with the blood that races into my heart.
Then I would hang it on the white wall
so that I could see it any time I like.
Who could have created this thing called
separation that causes me such death-in-life?

1324

It's been raining since morning
and the wind stirs in the forenoon.
How the rain and winds grow mad now:
I have a thousand leagues to cover.
What if I should rest a while?
It will be long before this day is done.

2277

After a rain the night before Cold Food Day,*
a spring tint has spread all around.
Even the mindless flowers and willows
have all burst into brightness.
How is it that my beloved, now gone,
does not return?

* The day falls on the 105th day after the winter solstice. The day is set aside to pay homage to the ancestral graves.

1261

How many kinds of wine are there?
Just two, clear and cloudy.
What difference, cloudy or otherwise,
so long as it gets me drunk?
In the moonshine and fresh wind,
why should I not drink all night long?

1422

It snowed during the night;
the moon has risen;
it shines so clear and bright
on the glittering snow.
Only the clouds on the sky's edge
drift to and fro.

2113

All grasses and bushes are buried under the snow;
bamboos and pine-trees alone are green.
What keeps them so verdant
in the thick of frost and snow?
Don't ask, you fool, they say:
It is our nature to be green.

Chang, Man (1566-1629)

Chang served three kings in a variety of ministerial posts. His life was criss-crossed with disturbing ups and downs. He traveled repeatedly between glory and exile. Finally he withdrew to his ancestral home, disillusioned by the political intrigues and conspiracies at the court. We have one poem by him.

2231

A boatman frightened by the rough seas
sold his boat and bought a pony.
But the road, twisted like a sheep's guts,
is more troubling than the seas.
After realizing this, he may not care for either boat
or the pony but rather start plowing the fields.

Chŏng, On (1569-1641)

After Korea's submission to the Manchus during the reign of King Injo, Chŏng retired to a mountain retreat where he lived out his days.

1972

I close my book and slide the window open.
I see a boat floating on the lake.
Snowy seagulls come and go
to what end, I do not know.
Let them be. Far from fame and honor
I wish to remain in their company.

Kim, Sanghŏn (1570-1652)

Kim attempted to commit suicide when he saw the country surrender and bow to the suzerainty of the Manchus who invaded Korea in 1627. The Manchus took him as a hostage to their capital. A series of protest came out written in the wake of the surrender. He has four poems to his credit.

3

Farewell, Mount Samgak,*
see you again, waters of the Han.**
Who would ever voluntarily leave
the mountains and rivers of this land?
And in these uncertain times,
who knows if I shall ever return?

* The mountains on the northern outskirts of Seoul.
** The river flowing through Seoul.

403

Listen, Nan Pai,* never give in
to injustice and brutality, though you may die.
The brave smiled as he replied.
You said it, my lord. I won't bow to death.
How many heroes since antiquity
have known tears?

* During the T'ang dynasty, Nan P'ai joined a rebellion and when he was arrested, he was subjected to torture but he never gave in.

Cho, Ch'anhan (1572-1631)

Skilled especially in composing poems, Cho served Kings Sŏnjo and Injo in various positions including a local magistrate. He has two poems to his credit.

2018

How many times has the universe been made and marred?
How many heroes can you name?
The ups and downs of a nation
are but a fleeting dream in a short sleep.
What idiotic spirits over there try
to sway us against us seizing the day?

991

I got into a household of influence and might
on the off chance of selling them poverty.
Since I had nothing tangible to offer
I did not bother to strike a bargain.
Instead, they asked for the mountains and
rivers, the moon and the wind. I said no.

Hong, Sŏbong (1572-1645)

Hong was involved in a coup d'etat and its success resulted in his appointments as Minister of Interior and then Prime Minister of the Left under King Injo.

1682

On the day we were drawn apart
we shed a flood of blood-tears.
No tint of blue could be seen
in the rolling waters of the Yalu.
The white-haired boatman said:
I've never seen the likes of this before.

Yi, Annul (1571-1637)

During the reign of King Sŏnjo, Yi was a local governor, a mayor and finally the Minister of Justice. He left us with one poem.

2017

Let me make heaven and earth my shelter
and the sun and moon a candlelight;
convert the course of the north sea
and sluice it into my wine tun.
Then I will meet Old-man Star* in the south
and live my days free from ageing.

* The star is believed to rule man's ageing process.

Kim, Yu (1571-1648)

Kim participated in the deposing of King Kwanghae and the enthroning of King Injo as the sixteenth ruler of the Yi dynasty. He was Prime Minister under King Injo. We have only one poem by him.

1195

If only I could cut down the tall bamboos
that grow on the shore of Hsiao Hsiang Kiang;*
bind them into a besom
and sweep away all the clouds hiding the sun!
But since the times are in turmoil
I am not certain that I can sweep them all clean.

* A river in the province of Hunan in China.

Chŏng, Ch'ungsin (1576-1636)

At the age of 17, Chŏng fought against Hideyoshi's army during the reign of King Sŏnjo. In 1627 when the Manchus invaded, Chŏng became an acting field-marshal. He has three poems to his credit.

200

Nightingale, why do you weep
in the bare and quiet mountains?
The Shu* did not fall just yesterday, you know.
Why do you continue to cry so sadly,
rending my poor heart?

* An ancient kingdom in China, it flourished during the third century. The last king was said to have been reborn as a nightingale after his death.

1190

Carting a wagonful of salt, who would believe
it's a horse that can run a thousand leagues?
Cast aside among pebbles,
the rarest jade often goes unrecognized.
Don't worry. There will always be those
who know its worth wherever they see it.

Ku, Inhu (1578-1658)

Minister of Justice and Industry under King Injo, Ku also served King Hyŏnjong as both Minister of the Left and Minister of the Right. One poem is left of his work.

1415

I spoke poorly while in the king's presence
and was ordered to step down.
Now with nowhere to turn for comfort
I have set out for West Lake.
In the night the sound of weighing anchor
amplifies my longing for our lord, the king.

Kim, Kwang'uk (1580-1656)

Disillusioned with court life, Kim left the office as Prime Minister for the countryside. Author of "The Song of Chestnut Village" which contains a cycle of fourteen poems, Kim wrote mostly in the tradition of T'ao Yin-ming, the pastoral poet and recluse of ancient China. He has 22 poems to his credit.

175

I am lost to fame; lost
to riches and honor.
I am entirely lost
to the wealth of worldly concerns.
Now I am lost to my own self,
why should others not forget me?

1399

There, snowy seagulls,
tell me what you are after?
You're prowling in the reeds,
aren't you, to catch the fish?
Why don't you follow my suit:
forget it all and drowse the day away.

2038

All my books full of dinning troubles,
I flung across the floor.
As I spring onto the saddle to return,
whipping my horse against the autumn wind,
no bird freed from its cage
quite knows how I feel.

2355

Has the yellow sea cleared?
The sigh of a saint to be born.
All the sages in the countryside
rally about to praise the peace of the times.
As for me, with whom would I leave
the beauty of nature?

1941

Scour the earthen pot,
draw spring water from under the rock;
boil peas into gruel
and fetch some pickled greens.
What can beat these two tastes?
I wonder if others enjoy this kind of life.

697

I borrowed barley to make wine from my neighbor,
unhulled grain a bit short of one mal;*
I had it ground, steamed,
kneaded, and then fermented.
Since I've long had this thirst,
it doesn't matter if the taste is sour or sweet.

* One mal equals approximately 5 gallons.

652

Has another T'ao Yin-ming been born
since his death and departure?
The chestnut village where I live
could equal the place where he resided.
Like him, I too have returned to nature
to work out my fate in the overrun fields.

620

How glad I am to see you again,
my faithful bamboo stick.
When I was a boy, I rode your back.
What fun it was then!
Now come out from the windowside;
lead the way and I'll trot behind you.

85

The rivers and mountains are at ease;
they've been put in my charge;
I am their sole custodian.
Nobody can make a claim on them.
No matter how sour-graped they get,
I will not give up to them my share of joy.

680

The spring breeze stirred briskly
to melt the heaped snow.
The blue mountains far and near
begin to assume their natural hue.
But the hoary frost behind my ears
refuses to melt away.

1071

The office of minister is an honor;
yet I would not trade the hills and rivers for it.
In a shallop under the moon
I fling my line into the water.
With this unworldly delight,
why should I envy those magistrates or governors?

1168

People of the world are
foolish bores, one and all.
They know about death
but do not know how to frolic.
Those of us here are in the know:
we have fun, getting drunk all day.

769

Idling beneath the thatched roof
on a long summer's day,
I dropped into sleep on a padded mat.
I was about to wake up
close to twilight,
when a voice from outside the gate
clearly said: "Let's go fishing."

1187

I broke off a thin willow branch
and skewered the fish I caught.
I was crossing a half-decayed bridge
when I saw apricot blossoms raining down
into the whole valley.
I lost myself.

2134

The moon beams on the autumn river.
I row alone in my leaf of a boat
and cast a line into the water:
its plunge startles the seagulls.
Merry notes of a fisherman's pipe
from somewhere buoy me up.

Kim, Yuk (1580-1658)

Kim served King Injo and King Hyŏjong in various positions including Prime Minister in his later life. The next poem, the only one left of him, presents the warm and congenial atmosphere the men of that age shared with their neighbors.

1761

When your wine matures enough to drink,
be sure to call me.
I will welcome you at my home
with blooming flowers in the yard
and we will discuss over wine
how to live carefreely for another hundred years.

Ku, Yong (undated)

A scholar during the reign of King Kwanghae, Ku was a local magistrate. One of his poems has survived.

916

After the blue seas ebbed away,
sands gather to form an isle.
Green grass assumes its color
when spring returns each year.
But why is our prince, once gone,
never to return?

Hong, Ikhan (1586-1637)

After the invasion of the Manchus, Hong was opposed to the submission of Korea to Ch'ing and so he was taken captive to China where he was killed.

1229
In Shou Yang Mountain the stream, the bitter
tears shed by Pai and Shuchai,
sobs sadly day and night
racing by without cessation
as if to regret their unfulfilled wishes
to serve their country with loyalty.*

* See Sŏng, Sammun.

Yi, Chŏnghwan (undated)

In face of the submission of Korea to the Manchus during the reign of King Injo, Yi retreated into the remote countryside. He left us with ten poems that express his indignation over the national humiliation.

218
The grass in the ditch turns
green in the spring rain.
It is unaware of our human suffering
but we envy the grass its natural state.
We cannot compare with a mere blade of grass;
we are riddled with cares.

1871
This little frame of mine falls freely
from heaven to the ground;
where submerged in lovely-hued clouds,
is Seoul the capital city?
Like windrows driven by a gusty wind
I do not know my way.

2228
On a day winds and snow rage about,
let me ask you, emissary from the north.*
What rigors of cold does our prince
suffer on alien soil?
Tears blind the eyes of his subject,
left behind living as if dead.

*Princes Sohyŏn and Pongnim were taken hostage to China.

Yun, Sŏndo (1587-1671)

Yun was the finest poet of classical sijo in the same way just as Chŏng, Ch'ŏl was the best in prose poems. Although Yun suffered from the usual vicissitudes of official life, yet as a poet he attained monumental stature as the greatest sijo master in the history of Korean literature. He left us with 77 pieces. The full texts of "The Song of Five Friends" and "The Fisherman's Song of Four Seasons," both written in a cyclical style are given here.

THE SONG OF FIVE FRIENDS

423

Let me count the number of friends I have—
water and rock, bamboo and pine.
How I delight in the moon
that rises over the eastern hill!
What else do I need
besides these five?

222

The clouds are pretty-colored, they say,
but they often grow dark.
The wind sounds clear, they say,
but too often it is stilled.
And the water alone is always pure
running without cessation.

157

Why do flowers bloom,
and then fade just as fast?
Why does the grass green,
and then wither yellow so soon?
Perhaps, the rocks alone
are immune to change.

646

The flowers bloom when it is warm
and the leaves fall in the cold.
Yet, pine, how is it that you remain
unaffected by frost and snow?
I know that it is because your roots
reach down deep into Hades.

332

This one is not a tree,
neither is it a grass.
Who ever made it grow so straight
and why is it so hollow inside?
I like it because
it is always green.

1816

The tiny object rises on high
and shines on the whole world.
Can there be any other light
that shines brighter in the dark night?
You do not tell anything that you see;
you are my friend, indeed.

THE FISHERMAN'S SONG OF FOUR SEASONS

Throughout the entire cycle, the poet uses two lines of nonsensical refrains: *Yoheave-ho's* and *Chigukch'ŏng's* and the like in the second and third lines of the original. In my translations these refrains are absent.

Part I. The Spring Song

1352
Mist clears from the bay in front.
The sun shines on the back hills.
The night tide has flown out
and the morning tide flows in.
Flowers along the margin of the bay
brighten the far off village.

369
The day is getting warm.
The fish leap in the water.
A few seagulls fly in and out
flapping their wings to lift and swoop.
The fishing rods are ready,
is the wine jar too?

679
The eastwind whiffs up briskly
and ruffles the surface of the water.
We shall leave the east lake
and enter the west bay.
The mountain in front passes us by;
the back hills come in sight.

1571

Is that voice the cuckoo's carol?
Is that green the willow-grove?
Fishermen's huts in the haze
glimmer in and out of sight.
All kinds of fish are leaping
where the water runs deep and clear.

144

The mild sunshine beams on the water;
the waves glide sleek as oil.
Shall I cast a net
or shall I try my rod?
I feel like singing aloud;
I almost forgot about the fish.

1136

The evening sun slants westward.
I'll call it a day and head back home.
The willows on the bank and the flowers on the shore
renew my joy at every bend of the river.
Should I envy eminent statesmen?
Why should I bother about their cares?

866

I will watch the sweet flowers
and gather orchids and gromwells.
What can I carry with me
in this leaf of a boat?
I was alone when I came out;
the moon keeps me company on my return.

2169
I get drunk and stretch out, napping;
my boat drifts down the rapids.
Lavender petals are floating around:
somewhere close must be a Shangrila.
How far away am I from the dinning
crowds of men and the dusty world?

348
I'll tuck aside my fishing rod
and watch the moon through the sky-light.
Has the night already begun?
The scop-owls disturbs the clear air.
Drunk with endless pleasure
I forget to go back home.

439
Will there be no days to come?
How long does the spring night last?
Let me walk back home to the brushwood-gate,
using my fishing rod for a staff.
This is just how a fisherman
passes his days.

Part 2. The Summer Song

233
The long imprisoning rain has stopped.
The stream is clear now.
I sling a fishing rod over my shoulder.
I can hardly contain my joy.
Who could have ever painted this
picture of misty rivers and piled-up peaks?

1469

Wrap the rice food in lotus leaves
and don't bother about side dishes.
I have my bamboo hat on;
did you bring my rush-cape in case it rains?
Mindless white seagulls overhead,
are you drawn to me or I to you?

709

The wind starts up in the duckweed.
The sky-light looks cool indeed.
The summer wind is shiftless.
What do I care where my boat drifts?
To the north bay or the southern waters,
any place will do.

814

If the waters of the lake are muddy,
can't I wash my feet?
I wish to go to the Wu River*
which may have been raging a thousand years.
I wish to go the the Ch'u River
but I fear lest I land the man-souled fish.

* The first allusion is a reference to the ancient Songs of Ch'u which speaks of washing our hat strings when the water is clear and our feet when the water is muddy, and means to take life as it comes. The second refers to the anger of Fu Ch'ai of Wu at the suicide of his subject Wu Tuan. He had the body exhumed and thrown into the Wu River in a sack. The third is to the belief that the souls of drowned men pass into the fishes, with special reference to Ch'u Yuan of Ch'u.

724
In the thick shade of the green willows,
the mossed-rocks look grotesque in the water.
When we get close to the bridge ahead,
don't scramble to cross it before others.
If we meet a white-haired old man
he shall be given the best spot to fish from.*

* When the Emperor Shun went to Lei Lake, the people there ceded him the best place for angling, thus presenting an example of good manners.

316
Completely lost in my delight
I hardly notice the day close.
Beating time on the mast
let us sing boatmen's songs.
Who will mind the age-old cares of man
as we row along amid songs?

1135
The setting sun is lovely to see;
soon twilight will appear.
The sinuous path over the cliffs
slopes down under the pine trees.
Orioles carole in the foliage
that greens on all sides.

771
Spread the net to dry on the sand
and let us take a nap under the awning.
You can stand the mosquitoes, can't you?
What does it matter if blowflies pester you?
I have only one worry left:
the traitors may overhear us.

860

Who can foretell that winds and waves
will rage during the night?
Who was it that said
"Cross the fields in a boat?"
The grass grown thick on the bank
is a lovely sight indeed.

1544

I look at my snail-shell hut,
folded in white clouds.
A bulrush fan held sideways,
I mount up the stone path.
Is a fisherman's life free or idle?
This is my favorite excuse.

Part 3. The Autumn Song

799

Isn't a fisherman's life pleasant,
free from worldly worries?
Do not laugh at old fishermen;
I see their figures in every painting.
The four seasons are all enjoyable
but autumn is best of all.

1226

When autumn comes to the hamlet by the water,
all the fish fatten up and grow sleek.
On the boundless waters we can enjoy ourselves
to our heart's content.
I look back on the crowds of men;
the further away, the better.

894

The fleecy clouds begin to rise;
the tree-tops call in the wind.
When the tide is in we'll go to West Lake,
then to East Lake at low tide.
Duckweed and water-weed blowing in plumes
are a joy along the edge of the bay.

299

From far away where the wild geese fly
mountains come into sight which I have never seen before.
I rejoice in my fishing;
I rejoice in living here.
The evening sun all a glitter
embroiders a thousand mountains.

1626

How many fish have I landed, you may ask,
those with silver-mouthed ones and jade-hard ones?
We'll make a bonfire of reedstalks
and broil some of the choice ones.
Tap the earthen jar
and pour wine into a gourd.

469

The gentle wind blows sideways;
we can return home with sail unfurled.
The dusk begins to gather
but out-of-the-world joy has not ended.
Red-tinted trees and clear streams
are the things I never get tired of.

2375

Dew glistens white on the leafage.
The bright moon is rising.
The Phoenix Hall* is far away;
who can I give this silver light to?
The medicine that the Jade Hare pounds on the moon
I wish to offer to the great man.

* The royal court.

119

Are heaven and earth each to each?
Where am I, I ask?
The west wind can never bear the dust this far.
What's the use of fanning it away?
Since I have heard nothing indecent,
why should I wash out my ears?

1541

Frost ices over my clothes,
and yet I do not feel cold.
My fishing boat is small
but how about the world of men?
Tomorrow I will go like this
and again the day after.

1218

Let me hasten to the stone hut in the pines
and watch the moon at early dawn.
How can I plow my way through
the fallen leaves in the bleak hills?
A white cloud pursues me;
my grass garment grows heavy on me.

Part 4. The Winter Song

221

After the clouds have broken,
the sunlight is warm and bright.
Heaven and earth are frozen up
and the sea is ever the same.
The boundless expanse of waves
spreads smooth as silk.

1887

Are rod and line ready yet?
Has my boat been caulked?
They say the net will freeze
at this time on the Hsio Lake and Hsing River.*
Nowhere is better suited than
this place for fishing.

* Both are in China.

1464

The fish have left the shallows
and swum into the distant bay.
Soon the sun will sink.
Let's go down to the sea.
They say big fish will bite
if the bait is right.

59

The snow fell during the night
and the whole landscape has changed:
the boundless spread of plate glass ahead
and jade mountains piled up behind.
Can this be a fairy land or nirvana?
This is not the world of men.

277

Forgetful of rod and net,
I beat on the boatside.
How many times have I considered
crossing the bay way ahead?
If only a gust of wind would rise
and whisk me across it!

1766

How many crows have flown overhead
toward their nest for the night?
The evening snow begins to fall;
the road ahead grows darkened.
Who will ever attack Anap Lake*
and clear the woods of fear?

* Anap Lake or Oya Lake was a place where Li Su of T'ang camouflaged the
movements of his troops by freeing flocks of ducks and geese on a snowy night.
The noise of the birds drowned the sound of the troops, and the rebel fortress
was conquered. "The woods of fear" refers to the nervousness of the retreating
armies of Chin in 383, who thought every tree held an ambush.

813

A solitary pine on the shore
stands straight and brave.
Do not fault the clouds that lower far out;
they screen us from the world.
Don't shun the roar of waves;
it shuts out the noise and dust of the world.

583

Russet cliffs and mossed rocks
surround us like a painted screen.
What's the difference if I have caught
any gaping fine-scaled fish or not?
Alone in my boat I am happy
in a rush-cape and bamboo hat.

1969
It's long been decided that
I should live in the land of bliss.
Who was it that wore sheepskins*
and lived by the Ch'i-li River?
Who was it that spent ten long years
waiting for a reign of peace.

* Yen Tzu-lung retired to Ch'i-li River and lived there in sheep-skins, avoiding the
court life of the Han Emperor Kuangwu. Chiang T'ai-kung spent ten years in
fishing shunning the Shang tyrant.

1398
*O the day draws to a close.
Now is the time to rest after a bite.
When thin snow films
over the scattered petals,
singing merrily we go up
till the moon sinks behind the snow-capped peak.
I lean on the window with a pine standing near.

* Here the song ends.

840
I take out my long-unheeded harp
and play on it, newly strung.
It meets me with notes clear
and sweet as of old days.
But since nobody knows my song
from now I'll keep my harp encased.

1960
When blow-flies drop dead,
the flyswatter lies useless;
when leaves fall to scatter,
beauty wilts and withers old.
The bamboo grove is bathed in the moon;
I am happy in the silvering light.

1266
Whether I am said or gay,
whether I am right or wrong,
all I have to do is
to improve my mind.
What else do I care about
except being true to myself?

772
The mountains sprawl in a long range;
the road is long, water sounds far away.
My love for my parents knows
no bounds, forever unexhausted.
A lone wild goose screams across the sky
somewhere far out.

1772
A cup of wine in hand I sit alone
and gaze on the far-off mountains.
Shall I be made happier
if my beloved ever comes?
No need for speech or laughter—
I am more than gay.

507
Who says statesmen can ever equal me?
Can the throne match my state?
Hsio-pu and Hso-you* both shunned the world.
They were clever indeed.
What can compare with this joy
I have in the hills and streams?

* Both were famous recluses in ancient China.

1045
Beneath the rocks by the stream in the hills,
I built myself a thatched hut.
People will laugh at me;
for they do not know me.
I am as simple as those rustics.
That's all there is to it.

924
After I had enough barley to eat
and greens to go with it,
I sported to my heart's content
in the stream beneath the rocks.
What else can I hope for
in life besides this joy?

429
I am a lazybones by nature.
Heaven knows it quite well.
Of the thousands of human affairs,
He assigned me nothing
except keeping the rivers
and mountains out of the reach of men.

83

The mountains and rivers are lovely
but I do not enjoy them on my own.
I know it's made possible
by the grace of the king.
I try the best I can to return his favor
but there's nothing I can do here.

1129

After the sun sets in the west
the mountains are tinted in splendor.
In the thickening dusk on all sides
the landscape merges into darkness.
Come, boy, do stay indoors;
snakes may be out creeping about.

986

Rain is falling, unfit for field work.
Shut the brushwood-gate and feed the cattle.
Will the rain last forever?
Get the plow and tools ready.
We can relax while it rains
and go out to plow when it stops.

827

Shut the lone door, the wind is blowing.
Put out the light, the night has arrived.
Let me rest my head on my pillow
and have a good, nightful of sleep.
Boy, when day dawns, come
and rouse me.

1606

Moon-rise Mountain is high;
the mist is only to blame, though
for keeping out of sight
the highest peak of the Heavenly-King.
Let it be. After the sun rises,
will the mist not clear?

2345

They say it isn't decent enough
to live on state-loan grain.
Pai and Chuchai are to be admired;
they never bent to starving death.
Yet, men are not to blame for a lean year.
Each year has a good or bad break.

Yi, Myŏnghan (1595-1645)

Yi served King Injo in various ministerial positions. He has 8 poems to his credit.

254

If my dream-road should ever
leave footprints,
the very stone path to your window
would have been worn smooth.
But I grieve, for my dream-road
leaves no traces.

2105

Fishermen on the river Chou,*
do not cook the fish if you catch them:
Ch'u-yuan's spirit still lies alive
imbedded in the bellies of the fish.
Seethed by fire in an iron cauldron,
his loyalty will never die away.

* In the state of Chou in ancient China, the loyal Ch'u-yuan was drowned by an intriguer. It was believed that his soul passed into the fish.

119

The sun set in the western peaks,
heaven and earth dissolve in desolation.
The moon glistens white on the pear blossoms;
the thoughts of you rise fresh within me.
O nightingale, why do you cry all night?
For whom do you pour your tender passion?

1594

I cling to your sleeves as I weep;
do not shake me off.
The sun has already sunk
behind the far-off bank.
When you light a flickering lamp in an inn,
and lie awake unable to sleep,
you will understand.

850

Well past midpoint of my lifespan,
I cannot return to my youth again.
All I can wish for from now on
is to stop further ageing.
Grey hair, you know what I desire:
age me as slowly as you can.

484
With a goosefoot stick I wander
along the green stream into the green mountains.
All the peaks are veiled in clouds;
the mist silvers every valley below.
I hope to come as often as I can
to such a place of wonder.

Chŏng, Tugyŏng (1597-1673)

Chŏng served King Injo as a Vice Minister of Culture and Education, but soon
retired from official life to live in the countryside. We have two poems by him.

292
A cask of wine was brought into the room;
I drank it to the bottom.
Song after song follows:
I grow merrier and merrier.
Do not say the sun is going down.
The moon will soon rise.

Yi, Wan (1602-1674)

During the reign of King Hyŏjong, Yi was the Director of the Royal Palace
Keeper's Bureau and then the Prime Minister of the Right. He distinguished
himself during the Manchu invasion. He has 2 poems to his credit.

243
Had I levelled Chun Shan*
the Tung-t'ing Lake would have been larger.
If I could cut down the casia on the moon
it would radiate an even brighter light.
But since my wishes remain unfulfilled
I regret having grown old in vain.

* A mountain in the middle of Tung-t'ing Lake in Hunan Province in China.

Kang, Paeknyŏn (1603-1681)

During the reign of King Sukchong, Kang was the Minister of Culture and Education.

2093

I was lovely and fair when young.
Now I am worn and aged thinking of you.
I wonder if you would recognize me
if we ever happened to meet on the road.
I wish someone would draw a picture of me
and present it to my beloved lord.

Song, Siyŏl (1607-1683)

Royal tutor to King Hyŏjong, Song was later sent into exile by King Sukchong for his opposition to the enthroning of a young prince and eventually was ordered to commit suicide by drinking poison. We have two poems by him.

580

I rose high in my beloved's favor
and I've trusted him ever since.
Now I am out of his good graces,
on whom does he rely?
Should he not have loved me from the first
I must feel much less sorry.

Chang, Hyŏn (undated)

As an official interpreter Chang followed princes Sohyŏn and Pongnim—the latter became King Hyŏjong—who were taken hostage to China soon after Korea surrendered to the Manchus in 1636. The next poem concerns the incident.

1358

After sundown over the Yalu,*
my lords, it pains me to see you
dragging your feet all the way
to Yenching ten thousand leagues away.
When the new grass flames in spring
may you return in no time.

* A 300 mile-long river flowing into Korean Bay bordering Manchuria in the southwest.

Chŏng, T'aehwa (1602-1673)

Chŏng served King Injo in the capacity of Prime Minister for seven terms. He has one poem to his credit.

1257

I had enough wine to get drunk,
now sitting relaxed and at ease.
Thousands of cares and worries are
anxious to take their leave of me.
Come, boy, pour my cup to the brim;
I should go and see them off.

Yu, Hyŏgyŏn (1616-1680)

During the reign of King Sukchong, Yu was a local governor and later the Minister of Industry. He lost his position in the Great Shake-up and was sent into exile to Cheju Island where he died. Like others in the middle ages, Yu was faithful even in exile to the king.

611

My prancing horse ages idling about.
My sharp-edged sword rusts unused.
The heartless months and years only
prompt my hair to turn grey.
I fear that I shall not be able
to repay the favors the king has bestowed on me.

King Hyŏjong (1619-1659)

The seventeenth king of the Yi dynasty, he succeeded to the throne in 1649. During his reign he attempted to rectify the national disgrace brought about by the Manchu invasion when his father was the king. We have 12 poems by him.

2038

The rain patters on the clear stream.
What is there to laugh about?
The flowers and trees
are swaying in a roar of laughter.
Well, let them laugh aloud.
How many days will this spring wind blow?

2071
Have we passed Blue-rock Pass?*
How far is Grass-rivermouth?
The north wind nips my flesh;
the rain falls without cessation.
Who would paint a portrait of me in this state
and send it to my lord, the king?

* A place close to the border between Korea and China. While a prince, he was
taken to Manchuria and held hostage.

Prince Inp'yŏng (1622-1658)

Skilled in literary composition and calligraphy, Prince Inp'yŏng was the third son
of King Injo and a brother of King Hyŏjong. We have two poems by him.

833
I was bent by the wind;
do not laugh at me.
The spring flowers swaying in the breeze
do not last in their beauty.
When wind and snow begin to rage,
you will envy me.

1903
The host is so merry-hearted as
he extends all hospitalities to his guest;
happy notes from a musical instrument
ignite my longing for home.
Indeed, peace seems to reign today
here in Milsŏng.

Nam, Kuman (1629-1711)

Nam held various government positions culminating in his appointment to Prime Minister during the reign of King Hyŏjong. Only one surviving poem is attributed to him.

677*

Has the east window brightened yet?
Already the larks are up and warbling in the sky.
Where is the boy that cares for the ox?
Has he not risen from bed?
When will he get the plowing done
in the long furrows over the hill?

* This poem is a realistic description of the countryside in past centuries.

Prince Nang'wŏn (? -1699)

A grandson of King Sŏnjo, Prince Nangwŏn was a scholar. He was skilled in literary composition and singing. He left 30 poems behind him.

1840

Content with what means I have
to live in a simple manner,
should I trade my thatched hut
for fame and honor and wealth?
Now I am way off from the dusty world
I can live as freely as my heart dictates.

2217

Idling away my lifetime
I wander over hills and streams.
The rivers and the lakes belong to me.
And no worldly worries badger me.
The rivers and hills, winds and moon;
they are, among others, my best friends.

1818
With my boy piper leading the way
I've come all the way to Maple-Peak
but the immortal hermit is gone
and the nest of his crane empty.
Boy, if you happen to see the Red-pine hermit,
tell him I am here.

732
We will never grapple with each other
unless we give in to hairsplitting argument.
No greed will ever plague us
if we do not shun discomfort;
labor done without good care
brings us no profit at all.

1050
The mountains stand as they are
but the stream has run dry.
The water flowing day and night
must have drained away.
I do not know if there's any river
that runs a thousand years long.

1385
My parents gave me life,
and nourished me with wisdom.
If it were not for them
I would not have grown wise.
I owe them infinite gratitude.
When shall I be able to pay them back?

Pak, T'aebo (1654-1689)

Pak held a succession of public positions including those of local magistrate and royal agent. Two poems are attributed to him.

2366

In my breast a fire blazes up
and consumes all my vital organs.
I saw Shen-nung* in a dream
and asked him for a remedy.
That fire comes of loyalty and just wrath;
nothing can extinguish it, he said.

* A legendary physician king in ancient China.

2070

Oh, pine tree in the green mountains,
how is it you lie so prostrate?
I have been uprooted,
overpowered by a raging gale.
If you chance to meet a skilled carpenter,
tell him it is for him I am here.

Yi, T'aek (1651-1719)

Yi held an important military position during King Sukchong's reign. He has two poems to his credit.

71

Roc-like giant of a bird, do not mock
the wren because it is small.
He and you alike traverse
the ninety thousand leagues of the sky.
There's not much difference between the two,
for both belong to the winging tribe.

Kim, Ch'ang'ŏp (1658-1721)

After a public life spent at court, Kim retired to the countryside where he spent his remaining days as a simple farmer. He left us with 4 poems.

115

The plectrum of my lute set aside,
I slip into a light noon nap.
But soon the dog barks at the gate
to announce a welcome guest.
Quickly, boy, fix some lunch;
and fetch some wine on credit.

1760

The other day I took out
my falcon, grown a foot long,
out into the slanting evening sun,
bells tied to its tuck-tail.
What greater contentment could I
ask for as a man?

906

What if all assume public office?
Who will sweat in the fields?
Have the doctors found a cure for all diseases?
Look at the burial ground thick with graves.
Come, boy, pour me some wine;
I will drink to my heart's content.

Hŏ, Chŏng (undated)

During the reign of King Hyŏjong, Hŏ was a mayor and a royal secretary. He has 3 poems to his credit.

1122
After a snowfall on West Lake,
The moon shines bright and clear.
I adjust my black upper-robe and
stroll along the shore of the lake.
It's so beautiful I fall into a trance
as if I encountered a winged fairy.

551
The straw-roofing's all pulled down;
can the hedged-fortress remain unscathed?
You have to pass the long night
in a room without heat or comfort.
Children whine and grumble;
they know so little of the world.

Part V. The End of the Dynasty
(The 18th and 19th Centuries)

Comprising about 170 years ranging from 1721 to 1894, this period saw Korea opening her door to the western world. It was at this period that the sijo first earned its appellation as it is currently used. Sometime during the reigns of King Yŏngjo (1725-1776) and King Chŏngjo (1776-1800), Korean literature generally commanded a wide-spread popularity among the common people. Most important, the initial years of this period were characterized by the compilation of the sijo, Kim Ch'ŏntaek's *Ch'ŏnggu Yŏng'ŏn* (Eternal Words of East Hills) was soon followed by *Haedong Kayo* (Songs of the East Sea) by Kim Sujang and *Kagok Wŏnryu* (Sources of Songs) by Pak Hyŏgwan and An Minyŏng. The latter half of the period saw the general decline of the sijo mainly because a new type of literature, fiction, began to grip the minds of the people with the surge of Western literary thoughts, with the nation being torn between the internal disturbances such as peasant's uprisings and the impact caused by Russo-Japanese War at the turn of the century, the sijo gradually withdrew into its shell, ending up being sung instead of new ones being created. Only a handful of figures stood their ground as champions to preserve the heritage of the sijo. Among them are Kim Sujang, Yi Chŏngbo, Kim Yugi, Kim Sŏnggi, Kim Ch'ŏntaek, Kim Sujang, Chŏ Myŏngni, Yi Chae, Pak Hyŏgwan and An Minyŏng.

King Sukchong (1661-1720)

He was the nineteenth king of the Yi dynasty. Two of his poems have been handed down to us.

2142

The autumn river and sky are the same color.
The royal boat floats on the waters;
a flute follows the beats of a drum as I
shed my thickly-coated cares.
May we soon rejoice in a reign of peace
with all our people across the land.*

* The king experienced continuous factional strifes in the court.

Yu, Sung (1666-1734)

During the reign of King Sukchong, Yu was a Minister of Industry. He has two poems to his credit.

57

The rain that fell during the night
has swollen the river that flows in front.
The fat fish with darkened backs
leap at the drooping willow branches.
Boy, go and get the net ready
and we will go out fishing.

2041

A lonely heron stands alone
on the white sands by the green rivulet.
How could I expect him to know
what I have long had in mind?
We do not differ from each other;
we both shun the dust and winds of the world.

Yun, Tuso (1668- ?)

Skilled in calligraphy and painting, Yun lived during the reign of King Sukchong.

1527

I flipped a piece of muddied
jade onto the road.
Those who pass back and forth there
think it's a chunk of mud.
Some day somebody will know better.
Jade, stay there the way you look.

Yun, Yu (1674- ?)

During the reign of kings Hŏnjong and Sukchong, Yun held various ministerial
positions. He has two poems to his credit.

2049

Let my boat be tied to the stone bank
and a net cast into the shallows of the river.
When I land a foot-long fish
I will slice it raw, glossy as snow.
Come, boy, fill my cup to the brim
and I will drink the day away.

Sin, Chŏngha (1680-1715)

During the reign of King Sukchong, Sin was a royal comptroller. He has three poems to his credit.

907

High position is something to be coveted,
yet it cannot compare with my state.
I spur my donkey, wayworn and lame,
and we hobble along to my country home.
Suddenly rain comes in showers
and washes the red dust off my robe.

1825

After the last night rain
the front hills soak up the autumn.
In the thick bean-flower patch
my hoe flashes by the pine torch.
Boy, I fear lest the fish escape, scared,
from the bamboo weir in the back stream.

Kim, Samhyŏn (undated)

A minor military official during the reign of King Sukchong, Kim retired to the countryside where he passed his days in communion with nature. Six poems of his work have survived.

183

Do not seek fame and high degree;
glory and disgrace halve a match.
Do not covet wealth and honor;
they are fraught with danger.
We are free and at ease now;
there's nothing we fear.

492
If I could hold back
the green willows and the warm spring,
I would pluck even my locks of white hair
and tightly bind them to a stake.
Yet, I let them slip by me again this year;
I could not stop them.

Kim, Yugi (undated)

Kim was a master singer during the reign of King Sukchong. We are fortunate to
have 12 of his poems.

1787
If I cannot achieve glory
and make my name as a man,
I will grow old in a decent way
apart from all the trappings of the world.
To what else should I cling
now that I am free and at ease?

1489
Today we'll go fishing in the stream
and tomorrow we'll go hunting.
The day after we'll have a picnic.
On the third day we'll meet for a lecture.
Archery is set for the fourth.
Each should bring his own drink and snack.

2157
Spring peach and plum blossoms,
do not parade your beauty
but think of tall pines
and green bamboos in mid-winter.
What can change their faithful hearts
that tower and spread so green?

422

Susceptible to illness,
cast far from the eyes of men,
I have forgotten honor and disgrace.
Indifferent to right or wrong
I only delight in falconry,
for I am free and at peace.

2193

I scale the high mountain
and look down over the world below.
Heaven opens up wide and broad;
the earth rolls on in an endless spread.
How my manly spirit springs
to life again this day!

Ku, Chijŏng (undated)

Ku was a local magistrate during the reign of King Sukchong. Only one poem is
credited to him.

1912

Oh, you kites that have pounced on some mice,
do not be proud that your stomach is full.
The thin crane in the clear water
may go hungry but will not envy you.
What does it matter if we grow skinny
as long as we are free and contented?

Chu, Ŭsik (undated)

Skilled in the ink-drawing of plum-blossoms and a master singer, Chu was a local magistrate during the reign of King Sukchong. We have 14 poems by him.

1952

A boy comes to the window
and says "It is the New Year."
I open the east window
and see the usual sun.
Boy, it's the same old sun.
Tell me when a new one rises.

1715

I ponder what life is like.
Well, it's nothing but a dream.
Good and bad alike are
all a dream within a dream.
So why don't we have some fun
in this fleeting dream?

2238

Don't dare to stand on tiptoe
simply because the sky's so high.
Don't stomp the ground
because it's so thick.
Whether high or thick,
accept the world as it is.

3212
I brought a piece of jade from Mount Hyŏng
and showed it to some people
but no one recognized its value
for it looked like a mere stone.
Why worry? Remain as you look;
time will tell what you really are.

533
Weak with age and illness,
I wish to go wherever I like.
Shall I stop on a steep hillside
and burn down a plot for a garden?
I do not expect to harvest much,
just enough to get by.

Yi, Chŏngbo (1693-1766)

Skilled in Chinese-style literary composition, Yi left official life for the countryside where he lived quietly in communion with nature. He has 78 poems handed down to us.

236

Chrysanthemums, how come you alone
are left in full bloom,
the warm spring wind long
gone and leaves fallen from the cold?
Only you can get the best
of the rigorous frost.

98

Do not envy the fish
that seem to leisurely play about in the lakes.
After the fishermen have gone,
the herons come to wait for their chance.
All day long the fish bob up and down;
they have no time to stay in peace.

210

Falling pear-blossoms whirl
madly about in the wind,
unable to return to their homes;
some are caught in spider's webs
and the spiders pounce on them
thinking they are so many butterflies.

1536

I will draw water into the paddyfield
and weed the cotton patch;
Dear wife, pick some cucumbers from the hedge
and cook that barley for lunch.
If any of the wine next door is mellow enough,
get some on credit.

26

Like a lotus-bud about to unfold
in the bright autumn moon
or a sweet-briar nodding off
in the spring breeze as misty rain falls,
I should say your beauty is un-
surpassed, you're at the top.

265

Return to the fields and again return
is a mere word, not the deed.
People think they know glory and fame
are nothing but a drifting cloud;
no one wakes up from the illusion,
and it makes me sad.

2216

It is my lifetime wish
to be reborn as a winged immortal
and soar into the blue heaven,
clearing away the clouds.
After that, nothing will keep the
moon and sun from shining.

166

When flowers bloom, I think of the moon.
When the moon shines, I think of wine.
When flowers open in the moonlight,
and I have some wine, I miss my friends.
When will one stop by
to drink all night beneath the moon and flowers?

1350

Nobody seems to puzzle out the mystery
of the creation of our universe.
Beyond the ocean spreads heaven;
what can there be beyond that?
Who said that heaven and our world are alike?
What can we do but to take his word for it?

33

After threshing the corn in the fall,
folks turn out for a village meeting.
To a high-pitched song of Squire Kim,
Farming official Pak dances with his shoulders;
the elder Yi laughs heartily
clapping his hands.

2122

What's become of my old master,
who long retired into rural obscurity?
He may be subsisting on coarse rice
and meager mountain greens,
a stranger to worldly cares, and I envy him.

1364

I come out to sit in a sunny spot
basking in the morning sun.
I wonder if this same light
warms the court where my lord is.
I have long had no news
from the Jade-hall* far away.

* Indicates the royal court.

252

I lay my head on my pillow to sleep
and see my beloved in a dream.
The candlelight flickers on the wall;
the duck-embroidered quilt is cold.
A lone wild goose honking
across the sky keeps me awake.

1755

Do not be pleased that you have gained something;
do not be sad for what you lack.
Those who lack do not realize that
to possess is to court trouble.
It is ironic indeed the way
everyone scrambles desperately for gain.

1723

The heart of man is as changeable
as his appearance;
the things of the world seem like clouds
lowering with menacing faces.
There seems to be nothing to do but to follow
the carefree seagulls across the lake.

362

The evening sun sets in the west then
rises again over the east sea;
the brown grass of autumn
sprouts green again in the spring.
How is it that man's life
never returns once it is gone.

805

Fluttering moths, let me ask you how you feel
when almost as soon as one of you falls dead,
another follows him and he again another.
Can't you see that your lives, though
they may not amount to much, are
headed straight for death?

681

Nightingale, weep no more:
I've returned at last.
Pear-blossoms have burst open
and a new moon can be seen in the sky.
We have rivers, lakes and seagulls;
I will see my wish come true.

562

Can any medicine cure this disease
caused by my love for you?
I sigh and weep tears
awake or asleep.
I shall not forget you
till I am dead and gone.

531

I have parted from my bloved,
whom I met in the afternoon of life.
There's been not a single word from him;
I wonder if he may show up in a dream.
He may not remember me at all,
yet how could I ever forget him?

1992

Snow falls on every hill and mountain;
heaven and earth are colored the same.
Can the White Jade Realm* or
the Lapis Lazuli match the marvel of this landscape?
All the trees have burst into blossom.
I feel as if another spring has arrived.

* A celestial world.

38

There, my lass, look at this flower
that blooms, then wilts so quickly.
Your cheeks are lovely as jade
but no youth stays there forever.
You will have regrets when old
and fallen in the world.

1495

The autumn wind stirs the paulownia
where rain drips intermittently on the leaves.
A swarm of worries closes in on me;
the shrill of the cricket makes me sad.
I fear lest the wild goose know
this part of the hills and rivers.

1001

After a man grows old and wrinkled,
he cannot recapture his lost youth;
his teeth, pulled out, cannot be renewed,
white hair never turns black again.
No herb of immortality is to be found in this world,
and that is surely sad.

2347

Can the waves of precarious court life
surge over this part of the green woods?
I pass my carefree days away enjoying
the rivers and hills free of charge.
The fleecy seagulls fly in and out;
they must know what I am thinking.

1037

When spring comes to the mountain abode
all hands are kept busy
making a weir to fish in the front stream,
or sowing cucumber seeds under the hedge.
When the clouds clear tomorrow,
I will go digging for herbal roots.

Cho, Myŏngni (1697-1756)

Cho served in a variety of ministerial posts under King Yŏngjo. The imagery of geese, frost and moonlight on an autumn night, used repeatedly in many classical poems, indicates homesickness. But the next poem had something more to say with its positive tone.

304

Wild geese have long flown away;
how many times has the frost formed?
The autumn night grows longer;
homesickness grips me hard.
But the moonlight that surges into the yard
makes me feel at home.

1147

On my trip to Mount Sŏrak
I met a monk bound for All-Bones Mountain;*
I greeted him and asked:
"What are the maple trees like there?"
We have had frost these days;
they are at their best, he answered.

* The Diamond Mountain is named differently for each different season: Pongnae (Sages Meet) in summer; Diamond in spring; Kyegol (All-bones) in winter and P'ung'ak (Maple Peaks) in autumn.

1156

The night deepens here in Sŏngjin;
the waves roar in the high seas.
The lone lamplight flickers in an inn;
my home is a thousand leagues away.
We've already crossed Mach'ŏn Pass.
What's the use of getting homesick?

2046

Leaning on my goosefoot stick
I ascend onto the Hapkang pavillion.
The moon shines on the valleys and the stream.
Only the sound of water comes to my ears.
Why is it the immortals on crane-back
cannot find me here in the night?

Kim, Ch'ŏnt'aek (undated)

A master singer of sijo and prolific writer, Kim was the first to anthologize classical poems in his *Ch'ŏnggu Yŏng'ŏn* (Eternal Songs of the Blue Hill), which contains 580 poems. He has 74 poems to his credit.

1540
I doff my coat and tell my boy
to pawn it at the wine shop.
Then I look up at the sky
and say to the moon:
Well, now! How about Li Po* of old?
How would he compare with me?

* The greatest poet of China during the T'ang dynasty.

2259
How many days a month
can I afford to get drunk?
The day I hold a cup of wine
is indeed the day for me.
After the day passes by,
who will encounter it again?

1775
Do not rush when you are well on the way;
do not pause when the going is slow.
Keep on your way steady and sure;
skimp on time to a minute.
If you come to a stand on the way,
you'd better not get started.

1704

Each facet of human affairs
is folded in the pale of fate.
Fortune or misfortune goes
in accord with heaven's design.
Other than this, there's nothing
for which I care less.

1167

Crowds of men, listen
to what I am going to say:
Youth does not last forever.
No white hair turns black again.
Life is a fleeting dream.
Why do you cling to it as if you live forever?

872

White seagull, don't be surprised:
let me ask you a question.
What famed scenic places
have you been to so far?
Give me their names
and I will come with you.

480

Reed-plumes grow thick in the valley
where twilight slants in a haze;
snowy seagulls glide by in twos
or threes criss-crossing at whim.
What has possessed you, I wonder,
that you do not notice me?

2230

Tied up to the dust and winds of the world.
I cannot forget and quit it clean.
But deep down I've long been
dreaming of returning to the countryside.
When I have repaid my king's favor
I will retire free of heart and mind.

1114

I have idled my life away
without mastering the books or the sword.
The fifty springs of my life
have all passed in futility.
Let it be. Will those green
mountains shun me for it?

381

Let me grow five different kinds of grain
on the slope of the south hill.
Even if it doesn't yield enough to spare
it will be just enough to feed me.
How can wealth and fame
be of any use to me?

1893

Friends luxuriating in power and rank,
do not boast of your four-horse carriage.
After hares are caught and killed,
the faithful hounds meet death for meat.
I am a stranger to fame or infamy.

135

Since antiquity no one has
surpassed Confucius in wisdom.
He traveled across the land
to guide people to light and justice.
But what can be expected of me,
a scholar spoiled and rotten?

84

If the beauty of the rivers and hills
is only for those in power,
how can I ever hope for them?
I am poor and powerless.
But there's no one to stop me;
I am gay in their company.

2334

The floral balustrade is streaked with moonlight.
Night deepens on the bamboo lattice.
I play on my seven-stringed lute
as I slant it on the cool floor.
A crane at the edge of the yard
starts to dance to the notes.

1178

Life is full of cares and troubles.
Let me go to the rivers and lakes.
The mindless seagulls will not say
anything if I come and go.
Perhaps, this is the place
where I will not have to fuss or fight.

189

What are glory and honor?
Disgrace often follows in their wake.
Let me have three cups of wine
to the tunes of the lute.
I will grow old, free and at ease
delighting in the reign of peace.

2047

I stroll onto the south field,
leaning on a goosefoot stick.
The paddy pollen drifts about,
the fish in the stream are fattened up.
Farmers sing joyful songs
on all sides, far and near.

1151

Who would recognize a winged horse
loaded down with brushwood?
I have been in the paddock for 10 years
and grown old to no purpose.
Somewhere a sleek horse
stomps neighing and whining.

2374

The white clouds and purple smoke
have settled down into every valley.
The maples tinted in the autumn wind
are lovelier than spring flowers.
The Heavenly Duke must have adorned
these hills just for me to enjoy.

27
In the long autumnn night
my thought for my love deepens;
the intermittent raindrops
on the paulownia leaves hurt me.
I am alone, it seems, to grieve
over my misfortune.

2264
When you are dead and gone,
no days will come around for you;
nobody will come to the remote
corner in the hills where you will lie buried
and fill your cup with wine
urging you to drink and enjoy.

1595
I have sown cucumber seeds
in the sunny spots along the hedge.
When the rain starts to sprinkle
I cover them carefully with earth.
This place is no other than
the field of Duke Tung-ling.*

* In ancient China the duke retired to the countryside after the fall of the dynasty.
He sowed cucumber seeds in the fields.

Kim, Sujang (1690- ?)

A minor official during the reign of King Yŏngjo, Kim compiled the famous *Haedong-Kayo* (Songs of the East Sea) which contains 568 poems and constitutes one of the three major source books of classical poems. A pioneer in search of new poetic forms, Kim devoted himself to espousing the cause of poems over the eighty years of his life. Some critics rank him with Yun, Sŏndo. 121 poems of his work have survived.

122

They call white what is black.
What is black they call white.
Be it white or black,
nobody says it is right.
I had best stop up my ears, close my eyes
and refuse to see or listen to any more of this.

536

Let my aged and sick heart
be a companion to the chrysanthemums;
let my skein of sorrows unravel
in ink drawings of grapes.
The white strands of hair under my ears
vibrate to the long notes of a song.

152

Flowers are about to bloom;
willows will soon break into green.
I have strained off my seasoned wine.
Friends, let's go out and enjoy it;
we'll sit around on the mountain road
and throw a welcome party for spring.

1821

The deep snow had already melted away.
Yet, I hadn't noticed spring's coming.
Homing geese wing across the blue sky.
Bending willows are alive with life
over the wrinkling waves below.
There, my boy, strain the new wine;
I will toast the on-coming spring.

775

Who can the master-mind be
that owns heaven and earth?
When and where was he born
into our universe, I wonder?
Nothing is known of his beginning
and end. He is infinite.

1751

When you happen to arrive in the heights,
do not laugh at the low land below.
Caught in thundering and howling storms,
you are apt to miss your step.
Because we remain on the level ground,
no mishaps will befall us.

161

Flowers falling, spring comes to an end.
I have emptied many cups and feel gay.
Time, like a passing traveler,
prompts my hair to turn grey.
What idiots are they
who speak against us having fun?

2319

Splendor is a mere make-believe;
wealth and honor are but a dream.
When the mourning hand-bell tinkles no
more over your mound in the burial ground,
all the regrets or repentences
of your life are of no use.

2076

Let the blue cloud be yours to enjoy;
I will rejoice in the white cloud.*
Go and seek wealth and honor;
I will be satisfied with clean poverty.
You may laugh at my foolishness
yet I will not change my present state.

* The blue cloud stands for secular glory and success and the white cloud for
simple living without worldly greed and cares.

2344

Those addicted to rank and power,
take care to consider the road ahead.
Like an innocent child who has slipped
out of his clothes in the sunshine,
what will they do then when the sun
sinks behind the western peaks?

1274

Let me grip hold of my worries
and bind them into a bundle.
Then I will hurl it into the green
waters that drift down below.
The bundle may be buffeted east and west
till completely dissolved in distant waters.

2330

At the north base of the Flowering Village
I have thatched my cottage roof.
It manages to keep out the wind,
the rain, the snow and frost.
When shall I take some time off
and bask in the sunshine?

1437

What a fool I am!
I am an impossible fool indeed.
To whom did I give my youth
keeping for myself only graying hair?
Too late now to get it back.
There's nowhere to even ask for it.

428

My life is simple and clean.
All I have for living are
a few grapewines and a volume
of musical scores for singing.
The companions most faithful to me
are the moon and winds.

2121

My grass-roofed hut is quiet.
Sitting alone, companionless,
I send my song adrift in the wind;
the white clouds are dozing.
Who else could imagine this bliss
I have all to myself?

1694

I am an old man now.
What else do I know?
Yellow chrysanthemums gild the hedge
and my black harp waits on the table.
From where it stands, my musical scores
are not allowed to lie idle.

1434

Hear me, friends, let's go flower-viewing
or fishing in the stream in front.
We cannot keep out the grey hair
that encroaches under the ears.
How far ahead our way lies
we will not mind at all.

1744

The peach and pear blossoms are a lovely sight in spring
the green shade and fragrant grass take the summer by force.
The golden chrysanthemums and tinted
maples grace the autumn. Among others,
we are most touched by the plum-
blossoms that open in the cold winter.

1959

Why is it that the green pine trees
laugh at the white clouds?
Why is it that the peach and apricot blossoms
are afraid of the silvering mist?
To me the pine alone is the sage, constant
before the change of seasons.

1060

I have no one coming to this mountain village
but I am not dreary or lonesome.
The birds chat to the smiling flowers;
the bamboos speak the speech of men.
The winds in the pines play the harp;
the nightingale sings tuneful notes.
Let it be. Who will mind my riches?

929

In the morning after a spring rain
I woke to find
a host of flower-buds unfolding
in ravarly with one another.
The birds cannot contain their mirth;
they sing and dance.

72

Girls are many in type:
some are like hawks;
some swallows on a clothes-line;
some storks in a yard thick with flowers;
some mandarin-ducks floating
on the green ripples;
others are owls perched
on the rotten stump of a tree.
None the less, they all possess
a beauty unsurpassed,
for they love and call for love.

766

The peony is the queen of flowers
and the sunflower a loyal subject.
The plum blossom is a hermit,
the apricot blossom a little man;
the lotus is a lady,
the chrysanthemum a sage;
the camellia is a poor scholar,
the gourd flower an old man;
the China pink is a boy,
the sweet-briar a girl.
Among them the pear blossom is a poet,
while the red peach, the jade peach and
the three-colored peach are young dandies.

Kim, Chint'ae (undated)

A master singer during the reign of King Yŏngjo, Kim associated with Kim, Sujang and Kim, Ch'ŏntaek. He left us with 26 poems.

1183

Months and years race by like a stream.
My hair grows grey with age.
I wish to weed out the grey strands
so that I will look young and fresh.
My old mother is still living
and I fear I won't live long enough to care for her.

1299

It is untrue, I think,
that there are immortals in the world.
How foolish of the kings of Chin and Han*
to never come to their senses!
Keep your mind pure and clean and
that will be the immortality you wish for.

* Emperors in ancient China.

1869
The oriole keeps singing, unable to contain
her joy, in the thick shade and sweet grass.
Her voice rings silver like a piece of jade
rolling down in the clear air after a shower.
Why have you woken me from my dreams,
as I pillow on the rivers and lakes?

1565
Great pine-tree sprawling like a dragon,
I cannot hide my delight in seeing you.
You've stood up well to the whippings
of thunder and lightning.
Who says the martyr, Song, is dead?*
I see him incarnate in you.

* One of the six martyrs who resisted the usurpation of the throne by King Sejo.

1783
O kite floating in the blue of the sky,
what are you looking down at?
Looking for food? I see you've caught
sight of a rotting rat below.
Well, if the phoenix happens to see you,
you'll be made a laughing-stock.

Kim, Sŏnggi (undated)

A master harp-player during the reign of King Yongjo, Kim liked to sing to his own accompaniment. He has 8 poems to his credit.

2327
Shaking myself off the dust of the world,*
in straw-sandals, a harp slung over my shoulder,
I take out my walking stick
and return to West Lake;
the thick flocks of seagulls in the reeds
welcome me as their friend.

* The second and third lines in the original differ from those in Chŏng's dictionary.

219
Who can take home an unbridled stallion
that runs a thousand leagues a day?
It may grow fat and sleek
on bean gruel mixed with bran.
But since the beast is naturally wild
you will hardly be able to break him in.

1521
I pluck a branch off the flowering
plum in a jade pot;
the flower is lovely,
unloosing a sweet smell.
I cannot bring myself to fling
aside the beauty, though plucked.

99

Cast out in the countryside, far from the world,
I keep company with seagulls;
I set my little fishing boat adrift
and play on my jade flute.
Perhaps, no other worldly pleasure
appeals to me more.

Kim, Tusŏng (undated)

A singer, Kim associated with Kim, Ch'ŏntaek and Kim, Sujang. He left 19 poems
behind him.

70

He went saying he would be back.
But once away he doesn't return.
I lift my eyes to see if he will ever come
as I pace along the twelve-balustraded hall.
The geese have all disappeared from the southern sky
and the moon slants down to the west floor.
And yet there's no news from him.
If he ever comes back home again
I will hold him so I can stay with him overnight.

1017

O love. This love of ours is a fishing net,
tied knot by knot, spread over the whole ocean.
Our love is tangled and entwined like the vines
of the melon, the cucumber and the water melon,
creeping all over the place. Indeed, our love has
endless miles to go.

Kim, Ugyu (1691- ?)

A master singer during the reign of King Yŏngjo, Kim was an associate of Kim, Sujang. He left 12 poems behind him.

1337

I press my children to finish the meal
then take them out with me.
We take our seats on a paddy land
where we lie pillowing on sheaves of grain.
As it happens, somebody near us
challenges me to a game of chess.

1973

Had I not known you at all,
I would have remained a stranger.
What is this love that shoots
up sprouts and fresh leaves?
When will I bear fruit?
Will you gather it all up then?

102

After a rain on rivers and lakes,
the water and the sky assume the same hue.
My fishing rod on my shoulder and the wine aboard,
I drift my little boat down the currents.
The white seagulls sporting in the reeds
are glad that I've come.

537

In addition to poverty, age and disease afflict
me causing my friends to flee.
When I prospered like a prince
I had many callers at home.
Now the only friend I have left
is this three-foot long stick.

Kim, Ch'iu (undated)

As a singer Kim associated with Kim, Ch'ŏnt'aek and Kim, Sujang. He has one poem to his credit.

91

Fisherman shouldering a net on the beach,
do not catch those wild geese* at play;
without them, who would carry messages
from south to north and back again?.
Living unspotted in an out-of-the-way village
could you escape the fate of separation?

* The wild goose is traditionally the symbol of a message-carrier.

Kim, Chungyŏl (undated)

A master singer and lute player during the reign of King Yŏngjo, Kim has three poems to his credit.

2284

When free, I sit alone,
my *komun'go** placed on my knees sideways
and practice scales on it;
then the crane outside the window,
listening to my music,
takes to dancing a spirited dance.

* A six-stringed traditional Korean lute or harp.

Songgye-yŏnwŏl (undated)

A singer during the reign of King Yongjo, Songgye has 14 poems to his credit.

1683

Look, my hair has turned
grey all of a sudden.
Well, there's nothing unusual about it.
White hair comes with age.
Why, let it grow white and grey,
but can this love of mine fade away?

116

I want to play my *komun'go**
but my fingers hurt.
So let me place its strings
on the pinetree by the north window.
There they will hum sweet notes
in the wind.

* A six-stringed Korean harp or lute.

715

I climb up as high as Machy'ŏn Pass
and cast my eyes far into the east sea;
clouds drift endlessly beyond the sea
and the blue sky spreads beyond the clouds.
The grandeur of the sight takes my breath away;
I doubt if I will ever see its like again.

530
When you are old, friends will leave you;
and, weak-sighted, you won't even be able to read,
so I will collect all
the melodies, both old and new,
and pass my days away, my lonely days,
delighting in sweet music.

Yi, Chae (undated)

Skilled in calligraphy, Yi was once the mayor of Seoul during the reign of King
Yŏngjo. Two of his poems have been handed down to us.

1106
The morning star faded, the larks soar in the sky.
I leave my brushwood-gate with hoe on my shoulder.
The heavy dew glistening in the tall grass
may soak my hempen breeches soon.
Oh boy, what does it matter if my clothes
get wet when times are good?

Kim, Muksu (undated)

Patronized by his seniors Kim, Ch'ŏntaek and Kim, Sujang, Kim was skilled in
singing and calligraphy. He has 8 poems to his credit.

358
Fallen leaves whirl about in the cold wind;
wild geese scream their way across the sky.
At the mouth of the river at sunset
I have just parted from my beloved.
Even Buddha and Lao-tzu could not have
kept down their tears.

Yi, Chŏngjin (undated)

Yi was a famous singer during the reign of King Yŏngjo. He has 13 poems to his credit.

786

When we send the old year off,
may our sorrows go with it.
With rice-cakes, bean-cakes and meat soup
served with new wine
we'll stay awake till the new day dawns.
Soon the monk starts his door-to-door
visit to collect rice: The New Year is in.

742

The black cicada chirrs "hot;"
the green cicada cries "bitter."
Do they say my wild greens taste hot
and my coarse wine bitter?
Rustic fools lost in obscurity,
we do not mind what is hot or bitter.

401

Though others scheme to hurt me,
I will not contend with them.
Patience is a virtue I cherish
and it takes two to fight.
We have only ourselves to blame.
What virtue is there in contention and fighting?

1904

Though death is a thing to be lamented,
it cannot rival age in sorrow.
When you are old your dancing arms flap heavily,
while your singing voice rasps in accompaniment.
Besides, you cannot even enjoy wine and women
and is anything sadder than that?

787

Locked up in my room I set to reading
for how many years I cannot tell.
The young sapling at the edge of the yard
has grown into a dragon-scaled giant pine.
How many times have the peach
and apricots blossomed and faded?

857

Cobwebbed hoops held in hand,
a batch of naked kids run up and down along the stream;
they deceitfully cry, "dragonflies, dragonflies,
if you go that way, you'll die; if you come
this way you are safe."
The kids themselves are in fact dragonflies.
Such is our life.

Kim, T'aesŏk (undated)

A singer during the reign of King Yŏngjo, Kim lived unblemished in the country-side. He has two poems to his credit.

1493
Will it ever stop raining today?
Wearing a rain hat, shouldering a hoe,
my knee-breeches tucked up,
I'll weed the paddy field
and then have a drink and relax awhile
before starting another field.

Kim, Yŏng (undated)

A son to Kim, Sang'yong, Kim was a Minister of Justice under King Chŏngjo. He has 7 poems to his credit.

978
White heron perched in an empty boat,
did the blue waves wash you clean?
So white in appearance,
can your heart be that pure?
If you are white in and out alike,
I'll gladly follow you and enjoy your good company.

521
Butterflies flutter like snowflakes over the flowers;
our wine gets cloudy before we can strain it.
To the thrumming of my instrument
the stork hops mirthful measures.
The dog barks at the brushwood-gate.
Boy, go and see if any of my friends have come.

Sin, Wi (1769-1847)

Skilled in ink drawing, calligraphy and literary composition, Sin was a Vice Minister of Culture and Education under King Hŏnjong. He has one poem to his credit.

807

Reverend priest, I want to ask
what the scenery is like in the east?
"Only flaming sweet-briars redden
the ten leagues of sandy stretch,
and snowy seagulls fly in pairs
over the distant bay through the drizzle."

Pak, Hyŏgwan (1781-1880)

Pak was a master singer and favorite of Prince Taewŏn, the regent of King Kojong, who reigned from 1863 to 1907. Pak is remembered for his *Kagok Wŏnryu* (Source of Songs), an anthology of 810 poems and musical notations which he compiled in collaboration with An, Minyŏng. Pak has 15 poems to his credit.

198

Nightingale in the empty hill,
why are you weeping so sadly?
Do you feel the pain of parting
just as I do now?
Is there any response
though you weep till your heart bleeds?

563

May my dreams of longing for you
become the spirit of a cricket;
may he enter your bedroom
on this long autumn night
and rouse you from the deep sleep in which
you have forgotten me.

661

With the spring goddess around the corner
everything alive fills with joy.
Grass and trees and insects
return to life this season every year.
Why is it that man never returns
once he is gone?

1117

The wild geese honk as they wing
when frost forms and stars spangle.
How far away you must go
that you fly even at night?
I have an appointment in the south
and I fear lest I be late.

256

My beloved who appeared in my dream
disappeared when I woke.
Where has she gone, where is the one
I love so madly?
Though dreams may be empty and futile,
I wish to dream of her as often as I can.

524

Who says the crow is black,
a bird of ill-omen and bad-luck?
The crow returns his parents' love
by feeding them when they are old.
Some people are not so grateful
as the crow and it makes me sad.

Ki, Chŏngjin (1798-1876)

When a mere child of seven, Ki was believed to have mastered all the classics. He had briefly served as Vice Minister of Interior before he retired to the countryside where he spent his days reading. One poem is credited to him.

174

Let glory and fame attend you.
Heroic hearts never move me.
The door shut, my room is a mountain retreat;
my books serve as my friends and teacher.
Though no place beckons me now
I will go when I have drunk this joy to the dregs.

Prince Yuch'ŏn (undated)

Great-grandson of King Sŏnjo, Prince Yuch'ŏn was skilled at drawing and calligraphy. We have two poems by him.

1418

Yesterday I was dead drunk
and again it is wine today.
Was I sober the day before yesterday?
I do not even recall the day before that.
Tomorrow I will invite my friends to West Lake;
if I stay sober or not I cannot say.

2139

The autumn mountains washed by the autumn wind
now soak in the autumn river.
In the blue of the autumn sky
the autumnal moon is moored;
a pair of wild autumn ducks wing
southward through the autumn frost.

Kim, Minsun (undated

Kim was local governor in the latter part of the Yi dynasty. He was a famous singer at the time. He has 15 poems to his credit.

392

I planted the flowers in the south yard
to enjoy a hundred years of spring color.
But a sudden gust of wind and frost at dawn
have blasted them away as quickly as they bloomed.
Bees and butterflies throng about for them;
they are at a loss where to go.

412

I have never known an illness
except for the insomnia I suffer from.
Till the lamplight flickers out
and the day dawns at cockcrow
I lie curled up, unable to get my sleep,
Continually thinking of my beloved.

Prince Ikchong (1809-1830)

King Sunjo's son and a father to King Hŏnjong, he left us with 9 poems.

148

Her walk in the moonshine is graceful.
The wind caresses her silken sleeves;
her winsome manner before the flowers
captures the heart of her consort the king.
Of all the delightful dances in the world,
the Dance of the Nightingale* is the best.

* A courtly dance performed at a banquet.

291
I offer your grace a jade cup of wine
poured from a golden flask
and pray from the depths of my heart for
your grace to enjoy a long life;
and the south hill to consider my wish
that each season will be an eternal spring.

An, Minyŏng (1816- ?)

An was a master singer, representing the last of the classical poets of the Yi
dynasty. An's poems are mostly concerned with his love for flowers and the
kisaeng. He has 28 poems to his credit including "The Song of the Plum
Blossom."

1383
Your boughs immature and gaunt,
I did not expect much of you.
But you've kept your promise
by flaring into a handful of blossoms.
When I come for you by candlelight
your subtle scent perfumes the air.

992
Clear and graceful as jade
you shine bright in the snow;
quietly you unloose your fragrance
to meet with the moon at dusk.
What can compare with you
for grace and fidelity?

520
You have blossomed at last
as if you made a promise with the snow.
The moon rises over the brushwood-gate,
casting thin shadows.
Sweet scents float in the cup
and I will enjoy getting drunk.

2301
After sundown, did the rising moon
promise to meet with you?
The flowers asleep in the room greet it
by loosening a fragrance.
Why did I not know before
that the plum-blossoms and moon are friends.

1847
Far distant in the snows of Lofu Shan,*
on the rough and dark stump of a tree,
what force has sprouted your branches
and burst you into blossom?
Though half the stump remains rotten,
isn't there embedded in it the sign of spring?

* Famous for plum blossoms, this mountain is located in Kwang-tung Province in
China.

743
In the window shadowed by the plum-blossoms
like a fair lady leaning, her hair fastened with a gold pin,
a handful of white-haired old men
sing to the notes of their harps.
Soon the moon rises,
and that pass round the cup.

660
Are those flowers hidden in the East Pavillion
rhododendrons or azaleas?
With heaven and earth submerged in the snow,
how could have they bloomed?
I can see nothing but the plum blossoms
that free the warmth of spring from the snow.

836
The wind has driven the snow
against the window of the mountain cabin.
Chill air steals inside
and attacks the sleeping plum-blossoms.
No matter how the winter strives to freeze it
it cannot crush the will of the on-coming spring.

202
On a night when snowdrifts madden the empty hills,
my friend is coming from afar to see me.
The dog barks at the brushwood-gate;
can you hear him, or can't you?
The snow has covered the stony path;
throw up the reins to the donkey.

237

Chrysanthemums, let me ask you
why you shun the warmth of spring air?
"I would rather freeze and die near the bare hedge,
in the cold after a chill rain.
I hate to mix with the host of flowers
that emerge in the springtime."

213

The orioles spin out a sweet song.
Do not envy the butterfly her dance.
You may think you will be left alone to reign
if there was no dancing butterfly;
but then no tenderness would attend you
without an accompanying ballet.

607

Flowers blowing inside the fence,
do not envy the glistening willow.
If the willow were not wreathed in pollen,
you would be alone to glow red and fair;
yet no tenderness would attend you
without the willow greening near you.

Im, Ŭijik (undated)

A famous harp player, Im left us with 6 poems.

92

Dusk gathers in the riverside hamlet.
The waters are dotted with the torches of fishermen,
and boats crowded the river.
Fishermen exorcise to the beating of drums.
The hills are wrapped in darkness and quiet
amid the splashings of oars in the night.

294

Aboard a boat on the golden waves
under sail with a clear wind
I steer toward mid-stream
and play my flute.
I start back home, drunk under the moon,
all my worries left in the wake.

889

On a day when snow swirls in thick flakes
bleaching heaven and earth
I wear a robe of feathers
and mount up the rock shrine.
Look! This the White-jade palace,
no other than a fairyland.

Yi, Sangdu (undated)

Yi was a local magistrate.

1902
The host will pour the drinks
and the guest will break into song.
A song for each cup filled up,
we will make a night of it
and when tomorrow breaks, we'll tap
a new cask of wine and drink the new day away.

Song, Chong'wŏn (undated)

Song has 9 poems to his credit.

1717
Everybody claims they know
life is a mere dream.
They do not know, it seems,
what they are talking about.
We alone are in the know;
we'll drink and enjoy ourselves while we can.

1139
Evening birds are returning to roost;
thin smoke spreads overhead.
The moon climbs over the east ridge
and shines on my dear old thoughts.
There boy, pour some wine into that earthen jar;
I'll play some music now.

2307
Sitting in a leaf of a boat
I fling a line into the green water.
Others may justly think
I am out to land a fish.
No sir. The best I can make of how to live
is to fish without catching any.

Sin, Hŭimun (undated)

Sin has 14 poems to his credit.

2096
How many years have rolled by
since we parted as youths?
Time flashes past as quickly as light.
Your pretty face is wrinkled with age.
My beloved, do not blame these grey hairs
but this life made for separation.

684
Separation lets one go away
and leaves the other behind.
When a longing for you seizes me
my insides begin to decay.
My beloved, stop to consider
if you really must go and leave me.

1935
Washing my hands clean of the dusty world,
tapping my bamboo stick on the path,
a lute strapped on my back
I enter the west lake.
The white seagulls float on the waves;
they are my best friends.

938

Wearing knee-breeches and shouldering a hoe,
I furrow the field and root out the weeds.
Humming a farmer's tune I return
with the moon on my head.
My wife strains some wine and says
the back field also needs my care.

Prince Chŏksŏng (undated)

1904

After an early morning shower,
Boys, rise from your beds.
Haven't the ferns sprouted
yet in the back hill?
Start right now to gather them,
a good sidedish for the new wine.

Pak, Hŭisŏk (undated)

Pak has three poems to his credit.

1773

The candlelight flickering over my shallow sleep
keeps company with my dreams, in which
I long for my beloved far away
at the edge of an alien sky.
The moon's down; the nightingale weeps no more.
The yard is covered with fallen petals.

O, Kyŏnghwa (undated)

O has three poems to his credit.

1902

When I wake up from a midday nap
to the persistent cries of a cuckoo,
I find my little son reading,
my daughter-in-law weaving cloth,
and my grandson toying with flowers in the yard.
My wife happens to be straining wine;
she tells me to come and taste it.

Ho, Sŏkkyun (undated)

16 poems are attributed to Ho.

251

I lie down and try to sleep
so that I might see you in a dream.
How the nightingale cries its heart out
till the moon pales at dawn.
It cannot be helped, for both of us are
gripped by the surging spring fever.

Part VI. The Kisaeng Class

In a closed feudalistic society of the Yi dynasty, women were not given equal opportunities in every arena of social activities. The kisaeng or entertaining woman, was, however, in a position to mix with the upper class or nobility, despite her low status in the social hierarchy. Unlike her modern counterpart, her trade was not always associated with an unsavory reputation of flesh-pot business. She had to be talented in arts and literature enough to match her male partners. For one, composition and singing of sijo became a necessity with men. Against the stock imagery and trite sermonizings most of the scholars employed in their writing, the kisaeng was free to express the naked truth and genuine feelings of man. Though the number of sijo ascribed to the kisaeng is extremely limited, amounting to as few as 60-odd pieces, over the whole range of history, quite a few of their works far exceed in quality those written by men. Some of them, especially by Hwang, Chini, merit the highest admiration for their artistic finesse.

Hwang, Chini (? -1530)

Apparently of high birth, Hwang was tutored by the great scholar Sŏ, Kyŏngdŏk.
Perhaps her unusual beauty and talent fated her to a life of a kisaeng. She left six
poems behind her.

1050

The mountains remain the same as of old
but the stream is constantly changing.
It flows day and night;
how could it be the same water?
The men of fame are like the stream:
once gone, they will not return.

1427

What have I done?
Didn't I know I would miss him so?
Had I but asked him to stay,
how could he have gone?
But I was foolish enough to send him away.
How I miss him now!

2063

The blue hills are my thoughts;
the green waters, my beloved's love.
Though the green waters flow away,
what can the blue hills do but remain?
No wonder, the green waters cry,
unable to forget the blue hills.

434
When did I ever lack faith in you?
When was I ever untrue to you
when there was no sign that you would arrive
until the small hours?
What could I do with the sound of leaves
that drift by in the autumn wind?

672
I will cut into halves the waist
of the long mid-winter night;
roll it up to be placed
under the warm spring-breeze quilt
and I will unroll it at night
when my beloved arrives.

2056
Jade green brook in the green mountains,*
do not boast your swift course.
Once you get to the blue ocean
it won't be easy to return.
Now that the bright moon** overflows the empty hill,
why don't you stop to rest for a while?

* Jade green brook is a pun on the name of a man noted for his virtuous deeds.
Written in a taunting tone, this poem is used to disarm the man.
** The bright moon is a pun on the name of the poetess, her pen name being
Bright-Moon.

Maehwa (undated)

Maehwa (Plum Blossom) was a kisaeng in Pyŏngyang.

1906
Should I cleanly forget and perish
or live ceaselessly yearning for you?
Not easy to die and forget
or to live and yearn.
O my lover, say just one word
and I will know whether to die or live.

1366
Into the deep night till day dawns
I turn and twist, unable to sleep.
I hear a bell tinkle in the incessant rain;
it tears apart my love-lorn heart.
If one would only paint a picture of me
and give it to my lover!

746
Spring has come to the old,
twisted bough of the plum tree.
Blossoms will appear unerringly
where they have bloomed before.
But since the spring snow is drifted about,
they seem half-minded to break into blossom.

1065
With my mind full of gentleness
and your heart full of tenderness,
we both ache to meet each other.
This yearning and pain I feel for you!
How many more days
can I stand being without you?

Hanu (undated)

Hanu was a kisaeng during the reign of King Sŏnjo.
The next poem was said to be written in reply to Im, Che's "Cold Rain Song."

1411

Why should you freeze in bed?
Why should you sleep that way?
With my duck-embroidered pillow
and jade-green quilt,
there's no reason to freeze tonight.
Since you have met cold rain* today
you'll melt in bed tonight.

* A pun on the poetess' name, Cold Rain.

Song-i (Pine)* (undated)

Song'i was a kisaeng.

1216

They call me a pine, everyone.
Yet what kind of pine can I be
but the one tall and spreading
on the cliff a thousand feet high?
The boy woodcutter may try his little sickle
but I am far beyond his reach.

* The pine is used as a pun on the author's name.

Kyerang (1513-1550)

Kyerang was a kisaeng skilled in literary composition.

1701
When pear-blossoms were raining down
we parted with tearful hugs.
Now an autumn wind knocks off the leaves
and I wonder if my love thinks of me.
Only my lonely dream comes and goes
a thousand leagues between us.

Munhyang (undated)

Munhyang was a kisaeng in the times of King Sŏnjo.

1492
Forget it. Do not say anything
if you do not love me.
Should you be the only man under heaven
you could justly hold your head high.
I will live with what heaven made me.
Is there not some who will love me?

Myŏng'ok (undated)

Myŏng'ok was a kisaeng in Suwŏn.

255

A lover seen in a dream
is not to be trusted, they say.
But I miss you so desperately.
And when can I be with you except in my dreams?
O lover, be it even in dreams,
I wish to see you ever so often.*

* This piece is sometimes attributed to Maehwa.

Kŭmhong (undated)

Nothing is known of Kŭmhong except that she was a kisaeng in Pyŏngyang.

915

A wild goose screams across the clear autumn sky;
I fling my window open.
The moon and snow fill the yard.
It also shines where my beloved is.
Perhaps I have been left alone in the world
to feel this pain.

Kuji (undated)

Kuji was a kisaeng in Pyŏngyang.

1800
I will shape the giant pine into a boat
and set it floating on the Taedong River;
then pluck a log willow branch
to tightly bind me to my lover.
Some jealous spirits from nowhere may
try to pull us into the quicksand.

Hongnang (undated)

Hongnang was a kisaeng during the reign of King Sŏnjo.

774
I pluck a willow branch
and sent it to you.
Plant it by your windowside
and watch it grow.
When buds appear after a rain
take them for me.

Ch'ŏn'gŭm (undated)

Ch'ŏn'gŭm was a kisaeng.

1062

Night falls in the mountain hamlet;
a dog barks from far away.
I push my brushwood-gate open;
the moon is suspended cold in the sky.
What sense is there in a dog barking
at the quiet moon and the bare hills?

Hongjang (undated)

Hongjang was a kisaeng in Kangnŭng.

2271

The moon shines on Cold-pine Pavillion;
the calm waves lap against Kyŏngpo Terrace
The faithful white seagulls circle,
gliding over the dark sea.
Why is it that our beloved prince,*
once gone, is never to return?

* An elegy for a royal prince.

Part VII. Anonymous Works

In view of the fact that more than 40% of 3600 pieces of the classical sijo known so far are anonymous works whose original dates of composition are uncertain, they carry a great weight in evaluating the sijo as a whole. Partly because most of the sijo were handed down from mouth to mouth until they found expression in written forms with the invention of *hang'ul*, and partly because the sijo by its very nature of being composed by a spontaneous inspiration of intense feeling of mood, the sijo form lent itself to anonymity. Furthermore, some writers preferred to remain anonymous in order to voice their political and social opinions unpopular with those in authority. Many of the love songs are veiled in anonymity also, chiefly because the strict Confucian ethics was hardly compatible with them. This section includes 102 poems.

484
Who will ever come to this valley
in the mountains where green waters run?
No one to sweep the petal-covered path,
the brushwood-gate remains closed.
I fear that a worldly visitor will come.
The fairy dog barks beyond the clouds.

1444
He is late for the appointment;
the jade peach blossoms shed their petals.
Can I trust the magpie that came*
and chattered merrily this morning?
To be safe, I'd better take out the mirror
and touch up my eyebrows.

* The magpie in the morning is traditionally believed to bring good news.

62
During the night the wind blew down
a gardenful of peach blossoms.
The boy servant is out
to sweep away the fallen petals.
Aren't they still flowers, though fallen?
Why don't you stay your hand?

377
The drum beats in the South Pavillion;
the Milky Way shines in the dead of night.
The boy in my heart
impatiently whips my horse home.
But no one waits in the silken window
and I am saddened by that.

597

O moon, O bright and round moon
that shines in through the window for my love,
is he sleeping alone
or with some other girl?
Tell me the truth, O moon
I am so desperate, so wretched.

738

I ride my horse into a flowering field
and his hoofs release its fragrance.
I step into theWind-spring Hall
which distills the scent of untapped wine.
Why is it that I cannot lay
my eyes on my beloved?

1180

On a drizzling day
clutching her purple cloak over her head
a girl scurries into the village
shimmering amidst masses of pear blossoms.
Excited by some false report
she's even oblivious of her wet clothes.

1396

I caught sight of him at last,
I've finally seen the monk.
His handsome looks and very body
fade in his threadbare robe:
a spring of camellia in the snow
flaring up against an ancient pine.

1574

My beloved roars like the thunder
and I greet him like lightning.
He comes and goes at a whim like rain
and we part again like clouds.
A gust of a sigh looses from my heart
and spreads like a silvering mist.

1023

What is love like?
Is it round? Is it wide?
Is it long? Is it short?
Can you measure it by pacing it out?
It isn't long enough to bind me
but it's strong enough to break my heart.

1955

A green wind-chime hangs outside the window.
I hitch a screen of peacock feathers to dangle below it.
When the wind blows, it sways
and makes a tinkling sound.
During the night I tilt up my ears;
it rings as if from a distant temple bell.

913

I have planted a paulownia
to coax the phoenix to come.
I wait but the bird is not lured by a tree
planted by an ordinary soul.
Only a slice of moon shines,
suspended on the bare branches.

831

O wind, stay, do not blow any more:
the leaves of the shade-tree may fall.
Months and years, stop and wait;
all the heroes and great men grow old.
What else can we do but enjoy
this reign of peace and quiet?

1404

Goodness, they deceived me,
autumn moon and spring wind deceived me.
Each season comes round in time
and I thought I could believe them.
But they left me with my greying hair
and set out in search of nimble youths.

2294

You sparrows chirping
at dusk after sundown,
half a branch is sufficient
for your tiny frame.
Why must you covet
the whole growth of such tall trees?

979

I think about the fan
and wonder why you sent it to me.
You must have meant it
to smother the flame in my heart.
But when my tears cannot do that,
of what use is your fan?

735

My horse neighs and paws to go
but my beloved holds me and won't set me free.
The sun has already crossed the ridge
and I have a thousand leagues to go.
My love, do not hold me back
but stop the setting sun.

1575

If we could be born again in the next life,
you as I and I as you
and you would yearn for me
as I have always done for you.
Then you'd know
the pangs I've felt for you.

1273

By the stream in the valley
I hew out a rock and build a hut;
I till the field in the moonlight
and lie down in the clouds.
Heaven and earth call me and say:
"Let's grow old together."

654

Peach blossom, why do you rouge
your cheeks, your eyes
brimming over with tears
in the misty spring rain?
I am sad because the spring
time passes so quickly.

1413

What kind of bug has
eaten away the great pine-trees?
Where is the long-billed woodpecker?
Where has he gone now?
When I hear the trees crashing down on the bleak mountain,
I can hardly contain my sorrow.

247

A grub grown into a cicada
flies away, its wings spread-wide.
You are free to alight and sing
on the top of the tallest tree
but you must be on your guard
lest you be trapped in a spider's web.

1873

I lost my fishing rod while dozing
and my rain-cape as I leapt in a dance.
Do not laugh, white seagulls,
at me, a silly old man. Way over there
the peach-blossoms glow ten leagues long
and I am drunk with spring air.

770

Red-necked mountain pheasant over there,
duck hawk perched on the branch,
white egrets watching for the fish
in the watered paddy field out in front,
if you were not around my grass roof
it wouldn't be easy for me to pass the days.

888

Heaven and earth are folded in white snow.
All the mountains have turned into jade.
The plum-blossom is half-opened;
the bamboo leaves glisten green.
There, boy, come and fill my cup;
I cannot contain this mirthful joy.

756

A dog barks in the distance.
How many travelers have passed by?
He should not have made a promise
if he could not make it.
I do not understand him at all.
Why does he not come to me?

488

A boy rides a cow down the bank
lined with green willows and sweet grass.
A rain-soaked traveler asks him
where he can go to get wine.
Over there where the apricot blossoms
drift about. Go there, and ask again.

1359

Fish in the pond in my front yard,
who caught you and stocked you here?
How come you left the deep blue of the north
sea to come and stay here?
Once in, you cannot get out;
now I see we are in the same boat.

674

Till the moon shining on the east window
sinks behind the west window, what keeps me awake?
When he doesn't come because he cannot,
my beloved has stolen my sleep.
What is the use of missing him any longer?

609

The boat sets sail with anchor aweigh.
When will you come back, my beloved?
I beg you to come back to me as quickly
as you go across the blue sea.
During the night the mere splashing
of oars slashes into my heart.

513

Can I get to sleep if I lie down?
Will my beloved come if I wait?
At this time of night no sleep
follows my lying down.
I might as well sit up,
awake through the long night.

124

Come winter I want the sun to shine
warm where my beloved stays.
Come spring I'd like him to taste
the tender and succulent parsley.
I know there's nothing he lacks
yet I cannot help myself.

117

I feel pretty as a flower
when I look at myself in the mirror.
How much prettier would I look
if I were made up for my beloved?
But he cannot see my beauty,
and it makes me sad.

66

Last night the wind blew open my door,
cunningly deceiving me.
So stupid of me to take the flapping
of weath-strips for his footsteps!
If I had said "Come in, please,"
even the night would have mocked me.

897

Try any plants you can think of
but I will not plant the bamboo.
The pipe weeps, the arrow bolts away
and the brush languishes in yearning.
Why should I trouble myself to grow that
which weeps, bolts and languishes?

5

Since he went away, I hardly see him in my dreams;
perhaps he's cleanly out of my memory.
I do not believe he has completely forgotten
me since our parting;
consumed with yearning for him
I reproach him in spite of myself.

19
Will the crow be black because it is so painted?
Or the heron white because it is aged?
Black and white are natural qualities
unchangeable since time immemorial.
Why does my beloved criticize me;
am I black or am I white?

1650
He seems forever false to me,
deceiving me this way or that way.
He is more wicked than my enemy;
it might be better to cleanly break off from him.
But the other day he gave me his word of honor
and I cannot forget him because of that.

109
The moon sets pale at dawn.
A lone goose honks across the frosty sky.
I am dying for news from my lover;
we have long been separated.
Only an empty voice reverberates
beyond thick fleets of clouds.

1149
Moon and snow fill the yard.
O wind, stay, do not blow.
What is it that I hear?
It isn't the footsteps I know for certain.
Longing and wistfulness seize me;
I wait for my love on the off chance.

534

Getting old and down with illness,
I cry my heart out toward the north.*
Nobody can easily quit and forget
without their heart burning for love
but I think I alone feel such pain
on this long moonlight night.

* The north indicates the royal court.

467

Where do you live, may I ask?
Up the stream across the hill,
you will find a brushwood-gate shut
at the edge of the greening woods;
a few seagulls circle down the hill.
Go there and ask them.

446

I live in the out-of-the-way place;
the philomel comes to sing at my hut.
Surrounded by valleys and folded peaks,
my lone brushwood-gate stands closed.
Even the dog does not bark here
but dozes while flowers drop their petals.

424

I am naturally lazy and not smart enough;
I have done nothing worthwhile so far:
not much to speak of in archery
nor in the way of learning.
I'd best withdraw from the world
and plow the fields in the countryside.

155

The night rain has unfolded the flowers.
The wine must be seasoned by now.
A friend with a *komun'go** said he'd come
to keep me company when the moon was up.
Boy, the moon is rising over the thatched roof.
Go and see if he is coming.

* A six-stringed Korean harp.

2171

Should we necessarily wear fine clothes
just to ward off the on-coming cold?
Why should we mind the mountain greens
if they ease our hunger?
Apart from these, there's nothing more
to ask for if we are free from worldly cares.

1866

Happy with the floating strains of a flute
I push my bamboo door open;
in the drizzling rain a lad rides
a cow down the bank of the river.
There, boy, spring has come to the countryside;
go and get my fishing rod ready.

1279

Let the dog bark at the brushwood gate;
nobody will venture to take the stony road.
I hear nothing but the sound of water;
I see nothing around but deer and hind.
How far away I am from the madding crowds
I do not wish to know.

105
Butterflies throng into my yard
bright with all kinds of flowers.
Do not dare to sit on a branch,
tempted by the fragrance of the flowers;
at sundown the wicked spiders lose
no time in spinning their sticky webs.

1170
People are made to talk, it seems;
they talk and talk and talk.
They refuse to see their own fault
but make no bones of faulting others.
They had better mend their ways first
before criticizing others.

703
Hold up to the mirror of reason
what you hear and what you see.
If it stands to reason, do it;
but don't if it is not reasonable.
Take heed of the language you use
and you will have no cause to quarrel.

2024
Let me collect all the daggers under the sun
and bind them all into a besom
to sweep away all the barbarians
on the frontiers of the south and north.
After that, I will beat the iron into a great hoe
and weed all the fields up the streams.

1997

Live for a thousand years,
live for ten thousand years
till the iron pillar flowers and bears fruit
and I will pluck it and offer it to you.
Oh, live again another ten thousand years
on top of the millions of years to come.

726

There is a Long-life well-spring
on Long-life peak on Long-life mountain.
This wine is branded Long-life wine
because it was made from Long-life water.
I offer you this cup of wine with the wish
that you will enjoy your life forever.

453

Do not do what you like to do
at the expense of others;
do not follow the suit of others
if what they do is unjust and foul.
We must follow our own nature
and do what nature ordains us to do.

737

My horse startles and shies.
I tug the reins
and look down into the water
where the green embroidered mountains are sunk.
There, horse, don't be scared;
I have come for this very sight.

29

I wish to cut off a slice
of the rain-washed autumn sky.
I'll embroider it with silver needles
and five-hued threads
and send it off to the palace
where my beloved lord resides.

375

I've never given it to others;
nor taken it from others either.
From where has it come,
this white hair, my hateful enemy?
White hair, you are not fair and just.
Why do you age me first?

1368

Like the tiny azaleas blazing red
in the crevices of the rocks on the East terrace of Yaksan*
you're so lovely; no one will pass you
without shooting a backward look.
I feel I've planted millet in the hills
where birds and rats come to plunder.

* A spot famous for azaleas in North Korea.

887

The white clouds doze beneath the thatched eaves.
The weary birds return to the trees for the night.
The chickens and dogs scattered about the village
add to the zest of rustic life.
Now I am lost to the crowds of men.
Who will ever come this far to see me?

1958

A shadow flickering on the window,
I ran out to see if it's my love.
But he had not come; a cloud was passing
across the dim moon.
How lucky I was it was night-time.
Had it been day, I would have been a
laughing-stock of the village.

871

Fleecy seagulls, do not take fright;
I am not here to hurt you.
Since I have lost favor with my lord
no place beckons me.
From now on no glory and honor will be mine
and I will keep friends with you.

1732

The blue hills recede further at sunset
Day is done; he hasn't come yet.
The cold is in the air; I am poor.
Does the chill keep him off, I wonder?
The dog barks at the brushwood gate.
Indeed, he is coming in the night of snow and winds.

811

A sudden shadow darkens the water below;
a monk passes by on the bridge.
"Stay a while, reverend sir,
let me ask where you go."
Just pointing to a white cloud,
he goes on without a backward look.

1828

When spring comes to the countryside
every one is being kept busy:
I have my fishing net to mend
and the boy is out to plow the fields.
Who will dig the medicinal herbs
that sprout in the back hill?

1042

Living as I do at the foot of the hill
I feel ashamed of the nightingale.
He pries into my hut and laughs
to see me so hard up and wretched.
Let well enough alone. I delight in poverty.
There's nothing more I ask for.

1382

Be a fool as any fool can be.
Be mad as mad as can be.
Half mad, foolish by halves,
half-knowing, half-ignorant,
casting about this way or that
I do not know what can be done.

1664

When I die and turn to dust
I will become a nightingale.
Hidden by day in the boughs of a pear tree
loaded with masses of flowers
I will flit out at night and sing
till my song catches my beloved's ears.

532

"I grow old, let's leave the world."
I have a talk with my heart.
"But where will you go
leaving your beloved behind?"
"Then, you, my heart, can stay a little while
but let me go ahead of you."

1309

After ten years of planning and work
I have a three-room cottage.
I have one room, the bright moon another
and the clear wind the third one.
There's no more space for the rivers and mountains;
I will have them stay outside.

1423

Again last night I slept curled up alone.
The night before that I did the same.
What sort of life is this, I wonder,
that I have to sleep, every night, curled up?
But since my beloved has come today
I want to stretch my legs and sleep deeply.

45

My sweet girl, I grab you by the wrist
and you toss me a beaming smile.
And I venture to stroke your back
till you warm up and embrace me.
Darling, please stop, no more;
I feel my heart bursting with madness.

360
Fallen leaves pressed under the hooves of my horse,
each looses the sound of autumn;
the wind-goddess turns herself into a besom
and sweeps them away clean and clear.
What does it matter if the bleak mountain path
should be covered with leaves?

2295
Toward the oncoming nightfall,
his unbridled cow wandering out of sight,
the herdboy with a handful of grass
heads where his legs direct him.
But all the valleys are veiled in mist
and he cannot find the way.

825
Even the winds and clouds pause
before they go across this pass;
falcons, tamed or wild, duck hawks and
peregrin hawks cannot pass, without a rest,
the steep Changsŏng Pass.
But should I know my sweet lover is over the pass
I would not pause before crossing it.

552
I try hard to forget you
but I cannot by any means.
Realizing my love is futile
I face the west wall trying to get some sleep.
But the wall becomes a mirror
in which you flicker before my eyes.

2012
Heaven and earth are an inn
for all creatures to stop in for the night.
The light and shadow of time are transients
passing for a hundred generations.
Life is a grain of millet tossed
in the middle of the boundless ocean.
Life is as fleeting as a dream. Why not enjoy it?

1289

In this time of peace and prosperity
I idle my carefree days away.
But for the cock crowing by day
from across the green bamboo grove
there is no one to rouse me
from my pleasant dreams.

1188

A blind man with another blind man
carried on his back, his bare feet
in clogs, heels knocked off,
stumbles along without a stick
on a rotten log over the stream.
The stone buddha down the road
laughs loudly at the sight.

1049

There are mountains and mountains
one behind the other far away;
there are roads and roads
forking off distantly from the main road.
There is no end to the mountains and roads
and I feel at a loss where to go.

1038

Surrounded by lovely mountains and waters
I built a cabin against a rock;
I go out to fish under the moon
and till the field in the clouds.
I can hardly make a living.
Yet, there's nothing more I ask for.

2275

May my sighs be a wind
and my tears a drizzling rain
that blows and sprinkles at will
against the window of my lover's room
and rouse him from a deep slumber
for he has forgotten me.

1142

Old man fishing in a boat,
with a wine jar perched on its head,
where do you earn your living
except for rod and line?
I've envied no one in the world
before I meet you today.

1669

When I die, do not bury me
but bear me in a straw-mat
and plop me into a pond of wine
leaving me afloat;
Then I will engage in my favorite pastime
getting drunk, without sobering up.

586
Maples turn half-red,
the stream runs clear.
A net cast into the shallows,
I lie down on the top of a flat rock.
Perhaps, I am the only person
ever to enjoy freedom and leisure.

1719

Do we have two or three lives to live?
Are there three or four bodies to carry us?
With this life of ours borrowed,
and our body bought on credit,
why should we struggle for a living
without enjoying it?

496

Down the long bank greening with grass,
herdboy riding backward on a yellow calf,
do you know of the noise and strifes
of the world outside, if I may ask?
The boy quietly smiles by way of an answer;
he just plays on his short flute.

1057

There is no calendar in the mountains;
I cannot keep track of time.
Flowers in bloom announce the coming of spring;
falling leaves, the onset of autumn.
Winter arrives with children coming
to ask for clothes, heavy and worn.

1124

The pomegranate-blossoms faded,
the lotus-flower releases its scent.
Mandarin-ducks are playing on the waves;
how I envy their destined bliss!
As I lean on the jade balustrade
a host of cares weigh me down.

589

A cup in hand I open the lattice
to see if I can ask the moon a question.
Its round and bright light
seems the same as that of old,
but since Li Po has long gone
no one can tell for sure.

156

Birds, do not grieve to see
those flowers fall and scatter.*
It isn't their fault at all;
the wind is blowing them off and away.
Why envy the spring
that causes such mischief as this?

* Flowers refer to the innocent victims of factional strife; wind, to the man who caused the disturbances; spring to those in power.

1914

The monk played the man; he stayed overnight
and left me. I miss him so. His pine-hat pillowing
my head, my bridal headpiece pillowing his, his robe
covering my body, and my skirt his. I think how
our passion ended in a pine-hat and a bridal crown.
Without him the next morning I feel wretched, my mind
restless and wandering.

1409

What shall I do? What shall I do?
O mother-in-law, what shall I do?
I was spooning up rice for my secret lover
when the brass spoon broke at the handle.
O mother-in-law, what do you want me to do?
There, my girl, don't worry so much.
The same often happened to me when I was young.*

* The poem is satirical. The image of a mother-in-law in this poem defies
tradition.

2040

During the night a green frog died of a bellyache,
a golden youth of a toad led the funeral by
saying a requiem mass;
a green grasshopper beat his hour-glass drum,
a black locust played on his pipe
and somewhere a crayfish under a stone
strikes his dance-drum.

475

Be a loafer. Loaf your life away;
loaf by day, and loaf by night
till the golden cock painted on the wall
flaps its wings, strains its clarion throat
and crows your head off.
Life is nothing but morning dew.
What else should we do but enjoy?

800

A white-haired wanton woman,
on her way to make love to a young lover
dyed her hair black, and pants and puffs
her way up to a steep mountain pass.
But she is caught in a sudden shower,
which turns her white collar-strip black
and her black hair white.
Her desire teases her out of satisfaction.

334

Butterfly, we'll go to the blue mountains;
you come along, too, striped swallowtail.
If it gets dark on the way,
we will sleep inside a flower.
If the flower does not welcome us,
we'll find a leaf for the night.

269

Cricket, O cricket, how I pity you!
Why do you have to cry all night
in tunes long and short under the sinking moon?
Your endless notes pierce and shake me awake
from a light sleep under the gauze window.
Let it alone; though a mere insect,
it alone can tell how I feel,
left to myself in my love-lost room.

330

Like a desperate hen pheasant chased by a hawk
on a mountainside without bush or rock to hide herself
or like a scared sailor on a ship on the high seas,
loaded with a thousand bags of grain, oars
lost, the sail in shreds, riggings cut loose,
the mast broken, and the rudder gone; the wind is
howling, the waves billowing, the mist thickening,
darkness is closing in all around the bleak expanse
of the raging swells, port is a thousand
leagues off, and when suddenly it falls to pirates,
you could not compare my heart with that,
when I parted from my beloved just a few days ago.

821

Brindled dog, black dog and blue shaggy dog—
Among the lot, that yellow bitch is a tactless wretch.
When an unwanted guest comes, she will wag her tail
and gives him a welcome.
But when my sweet love comes, she will brace up
her legs and snarl ready to bite and bark
her head off, you yellow bitch.
Tomorrow if a dog-catcher shouts
"Any dogs for sale?", I will tie you up
tight and sell you.

1271

Mother-in-law, don't be hopping mad in the kitchen
because you think your daughter-in-law is against your grain.
Did you fetch her in payment of a debt?
Or did you buy her in cash?
Father-in-law, cold and unkind
like a sapling on a rotten chestnut stump,
mother-in-law, skinny and dried up like
cowdung in the sun,
sister-in-law sharp as a gimlet
that sticks out of a three-year-old meshbag
and your son has bloody stool,
barnyard grass in a field of corn,
a cucumber flower faded yellow.
How can you find fault with your daughter—
in-law, a fair wild flower blooming
in the fertile soil?

667

The night deepens in the bridal room
for the consummation of love. How did I come
to meet this gentle and fair soul! I look
here, and I look there. I look up and down again.
She is sweet sixteen. Her face is a peach-blossom.
Gold hairpin and white ramie skirt,
bright eyes cast sideways
and lips half-parted in a smile.
Oh, she is the one.
What more is there to say about her silver-voice
and honeyed love-making under the quilt?

Selected Bibliography

Cho, Yunje, *Kukmun-haksa* (A History of Korean Literature), Seoul, 1948.

Ch'oe, Tong'won, *Kosijo Yŏn'gu* (A Study on Classical Sijo), Seoul, 1979.

Chŏn, Kyutae, *Han'guk Kosijo Munhaksa* (A Literary History of Classical Sijo), Seoul, 1971.

Chŏng, Pyŏng'uk, *Han'guk Sijo Sajŏn* (A Dictionary of Sijo), Seoul, 1982.

Han, Ch'unsŏp, et al., *Hanl'guk Sijo K'ŭn Sajŏn* (A Great Dictionary of Sijo), Seoul, 1985.

Kang, Hanyŏng, *Han'guk Sijo Obaek-sŏn* (Five Hundred Selected Sijo), Seoul, 1974.

Kim, Ch'ŏntaek, *Ch'ŏnggu Yong'on* (Eternal Words of East Hills), 1728, a source book containing 580 verses

Kim, Jaihiun, trans., *Master Sijo Poems from Korea,* Seoul, 1982.

Kim, Sayŏp, *Yijosidae-ŭi Kayo Yŏn'gu* (A Study on Yi Dynasty Songs), Seoul, 1958.

Kim, Sujang, *Haedong Kayo* (Songs of the East Sea), 1763, a source book containing 638 verses

Lee, Peter H., trans., *Anthology of Korean Poems from the Earliest to the Present,* New York, 1962.

Pai, Inez K., trans., *The Ever White Mountain,* Tokyo, 1965.

Pak, Hyŏngwan & An, Minyŏng, *Kagok Wŏnryu* (The Source of Songs), 1876, a source book containing about 600 verses.

Pak, Ulsu, *Han'guk Kosijo-sa* (A History of Classical Sijo), Seoul, 1975.

Rutt, Richard, trans., *The Bamboo Grove,* Berkeley, 1972.

Sim, Chaewan, *Yŏkdae Sijo Chŏnsŏ* (A Comprehensive Dictionary of Classical Sijo), revised, Seoul, 1980.

Yi, Kimun, *Yŏkdae Sijo-sŏn* (Selected Classical Sijo), Seoul, 1973.

Yi, Nung'u, *Yijo Sijo-sa* (A History of Yi Dynasty Sijo), Seoul, 1954.

Yi, Pyŏnggi & Paik Ch'ŏl, *Kukmunhaksa Chŏnsa* (A Comprehensive History of Korean Literature), Seoul, 1957.

Yi, Sangbo, *Myŏngsijo Kamsang* (An Appreciation of Famous Sijo), Seoul, 1974.

Yi, T'aeguk, *Han'guk Myŏngsijo-sŏn* (Selected Famous Sijo), Seoul, 1974.

————, *Sijo Kaeron* (An Introduction to Sijo), Seoul, 1959.

Index of Poets

Index of First Lines

A

B

C

H

I, J

M

U, W, Y